Hoodoo Spells of Uncrossing, Healing, and Protection

Khi Armand

Missionary Independent Spiritual Church
Forestville, California

✦ 2015 ✦

Deliverance!
Hoodoo Spells of Uncrossing, Healing, and Protection
by Khi Armand

© 2015 Khi Armand
http://ConjureInTheCity.com

Text:
Khi Armand

Art:
Charles C. Dawson, Charles M. Quinlan, R.C. Adams, K. Rudin, Unknown Artist, Charlie Wylie, cat yronwode, Greywolf Townsend

Cover:
Greywolf Townsend, Charles C. Dawson
(Lucky Mojo brand Cast Off Evil products label used with permission)

Editor:
catherine yronwode

Production:
nagasiva yronwode, catherine yronwode, Greywolf Townsend

First Edition 2015
Second Edition 2017

Published by
Missionary Independent Spiritual Church
6632 Covey Road, Forestville, California 95436
MissionaryIndependent.org

ISBN: 978-0-9960523-2-0

Printed in Canada.

Contents

Dedication

In memory of my brother and mentor,
Eddy Gutierrez, aka Dr. E.
(1976 - 2014).

We birds.

Acknowledgements

I would like to thank the following people for their help:

My dragon, Langston Kahn, for his continual support and belief in me. You are truly a gift from the gods. And a good editor.

Catherine and Nagasiva Yronwode, for including me as part of your family in these interesting times and for doing the work you came to do.

Prof. Charles Porterfield, for your wisdom, compassion, and faith in me.

Cat Yronwode, ConjureMan Ali, Miss Michaele, Kast Excelsior, Galina Krasskova, and Prof. Porterfield for allowing me to share your teachings.

Christina Pratt, for being a channel for the Cycle Teachings that have inspired this work, and for setting the highest bar I've encountered for what it means to be healer.

Saint Cyprian, for being my guide, tutor, and muse. Salve!

My parents, for loving me and helping me to know in a real, visceral way that transformation is possible and seemingly hopeless situations can be redeemed. The faith spoken about in this book is a faith that you embody each and every day and I've watched you work magic with it throughout your lives. Thank you, thank you, thank you for instilling that magic in me.

My Helping Spirits, for your eternal wisdom and mirroring back to me all that I brought into this life to share with others. Thank you for helping me shed old skins and choose fabulousness instead. It's preferable.

My Working Spirits, thank you for coming into my life by the strange, twisting, and fated avenues that you have and teaching me the beauty of asking, receiving, and of sheer devotion. Thank you for holding up my colleagues in AIRR, thank you for walking the paths you have walked, that you could share your wisdom with me and the world.

To the wisdom-bearers of yesterday, today, and tomorrow:

Thank you for re-membering.

About This Book

Deliverance! is a spiritual first-aid kit grounded in the tools and techniques of the Black-American magical tradition known as hoodoo, conjure, rootwork, and many other names, itself a testament to the power of endurance and adaptability in the face of adversity. It is a compendium of spells, workings, and recipes old and new, popularly known and innovative, including contributions from a variety of talented and professional conjure workers and root doctors whose insight, creativity, and commitment to public health carries forward the age-old legacy of forging connections between humanity and the guiding hands of the unseen into the 21st century. Without their wisdom and camaraderie, this book would not exist.

The spells transmitted here are a mixture of the traditional and the innovative. Much of what we know about hoodoo of the 20th century we owe to three people who made it their work to interview root doctors and home practitioners throughout the country. Newbell Niles Puckett recorded the spells of 400 named practitioners and published them in his book *Folk Beliefs of the Southern Negro* in 1926. Zora Neale Hurston collected spells primarily in Florida and Louisiana and published her interviews first in the *Journal of American Folklore* and later in the 1935 book *Mules and Men.* The indefatigable Reverend Harry M. Hyatt then interviewed 1,600 Black conjure practitioners from 1936 to 1970 and published his collection of more than 5,000 hoodoo spells in the five volumes of *Hoodoo-Conjure-Witchcraft-Rootwork.* To these folklorists — and to the men and women who so freely shared their time and knowledge with them — we owe an immeasurable debt. The present work could not have been possible without them.

History aside, most of all, this book is written from the perspective of a contemporary practicing urban American root doctor. In these pages I have placed an emphasis on modern-day applicability, accessibility of materials, and being in the service of healing (as I understand this word today). This book is the fruit of my own healing journey and work with hundreds of clients in my professional practice that emphasizes healing on all levels. Above all, it is intended for practical use.

It should be noted that many of the views expressed in regard to what constitutes well-being are my own. Not all of them are common amongst rootworkers or other spiritual practitioners, but they are the approaches I have found the most successful when working for myself and for clients.

Who Will Deliver Us?

*"...And lead us not into temptation,
But deliver us from evil..."*

—The Lord's Prayer

As a child, I had the privilege of growing up in a small, fervent Gospel-believing Black-American church in New York. Our congregation traveled to sister churches often to hear sermons delivered by pastors, prophets, and deacons all along the Eastern seaboard. With my head resting in my grandmother's lap at late night church services and prayer vigils, I watched scores of people walk with conviction up to the pulpit, convinced that something in their lives needed to change. From chronic poverty to alcoholism, abusive relationships to lack of purpose — each felt something stir inside, encouraging them to acknowledge an unresolved pain and ask for it to be healed. Each made the pilgrimage down that central aisle to the front of the room with the hope of being delivered.

It was around the time of my early adolescence that I was told I needed to be delivered from something stirring inside me. Though it was looked upon as a gift in ancient and traditional cultures, those around me believed it to be a curse, and everywhere I looked in my society, I saw echoes of their fears. People like myself had suffered tremendously for ages, but what remained obscured was that this suffering was not innate to our being; it was borne from the lies cultures tell themselves about beauty, power, and what makes people human.

Being young, I ate the lies up, praying and fasting in a refusal of the gift. I took many long walks up central aisles in humid rooms and under the canopy of large looming tents. I walked, many evenings, bearing a heart full of shame, toward the symbol of redemption hanging on the wall behind where the preacher sat. I tried to leave my burdens at the cross, but would awake each morning to find that they had followed me home.

It would be years before I understood that the lies I had consumed had torn me apart inside. A decade of self-denial and fear after an adolescence spent relying on others' ideas of who I had to be had festered into spiritual illness, leaving me vulnerable to intrusive energies. The real roots of the crossed conditions that I was experiencing were self-hatred, anger, and resentment. Freedom from these was the key to my deliverance.

WHAT IS HOODOO?

Hoodoo — also known as conjure, rootwork, helping yourself, tricking, throwing roots, and a plethora of other terms — is a traditional system of African-American folk magic both popular and infamous throughout the rural South since the beginning of the Transatlantic Slave Trade. Drawing on American Indian, Northern European, and Jewish kabbalistic techniques and tools at various points throughout its evolution, its roots remain steeped in Southern African-American folkways and the Congo practices of Africa that provide their precursor.

As an interconnected range of folk medicine and spiritual remediation practices developed and preserved by enslaved Africans, their descendants, and some ethnic outsiders, hoodoo fills a vital role in the social fabric of Black-American communities, where it functions as a primary form of counseling and healthcare while providing tools for protection and overcoming adversity in an overtly oppressive and discriminatory over-culture. By coupling the use of natural herbs, roots, minerals, and zoological curios with prayerful intent and traditional folk-magic methodologies, home practitioners and professional root doctors have responded to the needs and desires of their families, friends, and clients for hundreds of years.

Though couched in a Southern Baptist cosmology, variations of hoodoo have existed since its inception. One branch has Roman Catholic overtones, including the invocation of Saints. Another holds to veneration of figures recognized only in the Spiritual Church Movement, such as Black Hawk, the Native warrior. Recitation and writing of Psalms and other Biblical scriptures are popular practices, but do not override the fluid nature of improvisatory, Spirit-led intercession that characterizes conjure's Black Protestant foundations. Still, hoodoo is not traditionally considered to be a religion, making it incredibly adaptable to the spiritual paths of those who find it.

Today, many talented and skilled hoodoo root doctors have additional backgrounds in one or more other spiritual traditions and healing modalities found around the world, including Reiki, Wicca, Lucumí, Santería, and Haitian Vodou, to name a few. These workers' multi-cultural experiences inform their understanding of healing and of the world at large. Just as the early 20th century brought innovations, such as the use of candles and oils, from outside the Black-American Indian context, so will these eclectic traditions influence the practice of hoodoo rootwork for centuries to come.

THE TERMINOLOGY OF CONJURE

Hoodoo folk magic has developed a terminology and vocabulary that sets it slightly apart from other forms of practice. This list covers the most common terms, plus a few based in my own style or working.

- **Ancestral Helping Spirits:** A term popularized by Christina Pratt of the Last Mask Center for Shamanic Healing, this refers to our biological Ancestors who lived well, died well, made it to the ancestral realms, and have chosen to come back and walk with us, wielding the full breadth of wisdom gleaned from their lives. This is in contrast to Ancestors whose lives remain unresolved and have therefore not "moved on."
- **Anointing, Dressing, Fixing:** The application of oils, sachet powders, or herbs to a candle, petition paper, object, or one's body so as to imbue it with the essence thereof; the preparation of an object for spell-work.
- **Condition:** A state of being, or a product that aims to effect a state of being. Supplies are often named for the conditions they address.
- **Condition Oils, Incenses, Powders, and Baths:** Preparations consisting of herbal, mineral, or zoological curios intended to shift one into a condition that is identified with the product's named intents. Oils are used to dress and anoint, incenses for suffumigating, powders for sprinkling and dusting, and baths for personal bathing and floor washing.
- **Crossed Conditions:** A term that signifies a person's life is under duress. Remediation consists of uncrossing, jinx-breaking, or cleaning.
- **Curio:** An item used in conjure for its spiritual value and influence in prayers, spells, or workings. Curios include natural materials such as plants, minerals, and animalia, but also beads, coins, dollar bills, and amulets, as per the spell and at the discretion of the worker.
- **Curse:** An imprecatory spell or prayer to cause loss, harm, pain, or death.
- **Divination, Reading:** The intentional use of techniques, such as scrying, or tools, such as cards or bones, to discern information that is not readily available to the conscious mind or perceptible via the physical senses. Most conjure doctors are also readers and use some form of divination to help diagnose client conditions and prescribe acts of remediation.
- **Helping Spirits:** The beneficial, God-given helping and teaching spirits that accompany each of us during our lives, including Ancestral Helping Spirits, animal spirits, spirit guides, religious entities, and others.

- **Herbs, Roots, and Zoological Curios:** Items found in nature that are used by themselves and in condition-oriented spiritual supply products.
- **Holy Powers:** Archangels, angels, saints, and other divine spirits.
- **Jinx:** A mild curse or a crossed condition that kills one's good luck.
- **Lights, or Setting of Lights:** A hoodoo candle spell method developed in 20th century Spiritualist churches in which a fixed and prayed-over candle is lit for oneself or a client; it may be set atop a petition paper.
- **Loading:** Inserting petitions and personal concerns into dolls or candles.
- **Mojo Bag, Hand, Toby, Trick Bag:** A pouch or packet containing personal concerns and curios; it is fed and kept secret by its owner.
- **Nature:** Sexual vitality or libido; tying someone's nature is a curse.
- **Personal Concerns:** Ephemeral traces of people used to form links to them in spiritual work. These include photographs, handwriting, hair and nail clippings, worn clothing, bodily fluids, and foot-tracks.
- **Petition Paper, Name Paper, Prayer Paper:** A paper upon which one has written a name or an intention, often in a formulaic manner.
- **Root Doctor, Conjure Doctor, Rootworker:** A professional practitioner within the hoodoo magical tradition; one who works with clients.
- **Saints:** Holy people whose lives have been exemplary.
- **Spiritworker:** A practitioner who primarily works with spirits.
- **Washes, Waters, and Colognes:** Alcohol- and water-based liquid preparations used for cleaning, as altar offerings, and in spell work.
- **Uncrossing, Jinx Killer, Block Buster, Road Opener:** Spells, supplies, and prayers to remove evil and restore health, wealth, love, and luck.

ON THE PURCHASE OF SPIRITUAL PRODUCTS

Commercial spiritual products are staple, though varying, formulas for spiritual condition oils, baths, powders, incenses, and sprays. They may be purchased, just as you would purchase household goods or groceries.

It should be noted that not all suppliers of these goods use real plant, mineral, or animal materials in their products. Cheap, factory-made supplies contain petroleum oil or water, dye, synthetic perfumes, and toxic phthalates.

On the other hand, suppliers of traditional hoodoo products who do use actual plant, mineral, and zoological materials in their formulas often say so proudly, and the difference in both scent and efficacy is marked. I encourage the support of suppliers who make their goods by hand, not in factories.

ON BOTANICALS, MINERALS, AND ANIMAL CURIOS

Since ancient times, the Doctrine of Signatures has been used to attribute medicinal and magical properties to plants, asserting that their appearance holds a clue as to how they can aid humankind in one or more of life's arenas. The heart-shaped leaves of the Violet tell us that it lends itself to healing the heart, and the resemblance of Eyebright's flowers to eyes has resulted in the plant's use in folk remedies to treat infections in that part of the body. But the Doctrine of Signatures is not the only method by which humans have come to know the potential remediating properties of plants and other curios.

Folk magic embraces an animistic worldview in which all beings are deemed sentient and capable of communication. Those who work with plants often speak of the personality that each one has, evident not only in its appearance, but in the way it grows, how it interacts with other plants, and the way it behaves when utilized in medicine or magic. Hoodoo root doctors will place items in an alligator claw, combining lore around the animal's experience of luckiness with the tactile gesture of grasping and holding. Indian head cents of the 19th and 20th centuries are used as "scouts" that can warn when danger is near, drawing on early observations of Native American tribesmen as expert trackers. All things carry a spirit within them and by combining traditional lore with the subtle language in which objects speak, we come to understand their perspective beyond mundane descriptions and to enter into relationships with the spirits of curios themselves.

A curio's perspective on a condition governs how it will affect a situation and whether it is appropriate for a given spell. Like a sentient being, each curio offers insights on spiritual cleansing, protection, love, and vitality, even if it is not known to be "used" in treating certain conditions. One of my own teachers had a particular affinity with Bay Laurel and found it helpful in far more works than I did, whereas I've been encouraged by the plant to make use of it in spells for which I did not originally believe it suitable. That being said, no list of plant and curio associations within the hoodoo tradition is meant to be exhaustive. Every practitioner cultivates a relationship with curios that results in an intuitive sense that no book or teacher can provide.

Read more about botanical, mineral, and zoological curios online at **HerbMagic.com by catherine yronwode**
For more information on natural curios, see the book:
"Hoodoo Herb and Root Magic" by catherine yronwode

Diagnosing Spiritual Problems

In order to perform effective healing and remediation of jinxes, crossed conditions, and curses, we first need to understand the many routes by which such negative situations can come about, and how to distinguish one condition from another so that we may select the most beneficial treatment.

UNDERSTANDING MAGIC

Magic spells — that is, techniques used to effect change in the world through non-ordinary means — have been practiced in all cultures since the dawn of time, and as many variations in spells exist as do cultures that have ever populated planet Earth. Both spiritual specialists and laypersons have equipped themselves with knowledge and tools to help themselves and others.

Gestures, chants, incantations, symbols, mental projection, materials found in nature, invocation of spirits, and more have been used as stand-alone acts of magic and in combination with one another to ward off harmful influences, attract material abundance, encourage fertility, find lost items, attack foes, and achieve every other need and goal known to man. The belief that a magic spell's efficacy can be increased by proper location or timing is nearly universal as well, so some hoodoo practitioners enjoy doing their work by the signs or phases of the moon or on days ruled by particular planets whose influence is in alignment with what they seek to accomplish.

Newcomers to magical practice often wonder what the most "powerful spell" is for a given condition, not realizing that it's generally not that simple. A person's geographic location, ability to harness mental focus, the vulnerability of a possible target, and many other factors matter in terms of achieving favourable outcomes. Spells exist and can be invented for nearly every kind of circumstance, but a basic understanding of magical theory can go a long way toward quenching doubt and anxiety.

I believe that every spell, like every mundane word, act, and gesture, is a signal sent out into the Universe. As magic is most often performed to shift the odds in favour of a goal being achieved or the likelihood of an event happening, it is common for folks to be oblivious when a spell they have performed or hired others to perform has taken effect. Rather than being supernatural, magic works by bending the natural world to the will of its wielder, so its results are, more often than not, seemingly coincidental.

No matter what your personal goals, here are a few advisory guidelines for harnessing the energies of magic. These are not specific to hoodoo, but can be found in one form or another in many magical traditions:

- **Focus:** Focus only on what you want. To fret about what you do not want or to craft a list of outcomes you hope to avoid makes those things primary, and can be a sign of chronic negative thinking.
- **Specificity:** A clear statement of one's intended outcome yields the most favourable results. Praying for "a job" when a certain income is needed to support your family might result in a job that pays less than needed. As the Biblical God said to his prophet in Habakkuk 2:2, *"Write the vision, and make it plain upon tables, that he may run that readeth it."*
- **Openness:** Stay open to possibilities. There is a widespread belief that God, the Universe, Helping Spirits, and other Holy Powers want what's best for us while also being willing to respond to our desires. Performing a spell for a mate who is emotionally available and with whom you have great chemistry should suffice. Demanding that they be a coworker or come from a specific background might limit the possible avenues for that which you truly seek to manifest.
- **Communication:** Magic takes place within an animist worldview — the belief that all things are alive and conscious. Communicating intention and gratitude to the herbs, roots, minerals, and zoological curios worked with engages them on your behalf beyond rote inclusion due to correspondence.
- **Trust:** Catch-phrases like "Set it and forget it," "Lay your trick, walk away, and don't look back," or "Let go and let God" express the concept that after making your needs and desires known, you should trust the process and not succumb to second-guessing the outcome of the work.
- **Action:** Magic shifts odds and can increase the chances of our achieving our goals, but we must take action. A love spell followed by nights spent alone at home rather than out in a public venue to see and be seen is a waste of time. God helps those who help themselves.
- **Serendipity:** A spell performed to attract a lover may result in you missing your bus only to catch the later one and finding yourself seated next to a suitable dating partner whom you wouldn't have otherwise met.
- **Signs and Omens:** Be aware of coincidences and synchronicities which may indicate that the Universe is aligning to fulfil your requests.

UNDERSTANDING SPIRITUAL GIFTS

Despite the Western world-cultures headlong embrace of materiality and scepticism, quite a few people continue to be born with heightened spiritual sensitivity, or "spiritual gifts." All indigenous and indigenous-derived diasporic communities recognize such gifts; the terms used here are those found in the Black-American community to describe the kinds of spiritual giftedness that may be bestowed upon certain individuals:

- **Dreaming true:** Having dreams that give insight into unknown matters.
- **Having the sight:** Able to experience clairvoyance, having the ability to see spirits and disincarnate entities.
- **Being gifted for the work:** Having a talent to affect the world through conscious magical effort and subconscious manifestation.

Though innumerable books have been written about cultivating intuition, increasing skills in mediumship, and gaining spiritual power, little to nothing has been written about merely accepting spiritual gifts. Occasionally, when clients come to root doctors to ameliorate crossed conditions, the messages from their spirits have more to do with the need for them to honour and claim their own giftedness for the work than with curses. Mention of these gifts by the conjure doctor is often met with meek affirmation by the client, but the affirmation may be couched in fear and backed by memories of confusing childhood experiences in the spirit realm followed by negation on the part of parents who did not know what to make of their child's experiences.

Denial of your spiritual gifts — as with self-denial in all its forms — is far more dangerous than what you imagines acceptance of them will bring. You may not know how to use the gifts that you have incarnated with, but trying to shut them off or ignore them is akin to trying to run while sawing off your leg. Spiritual gifts are innate to our being, and I've provided many with divinatory messages in which the remediating actions toward getting a grip on life and gaining mastery, power, clarity, and sanity were to fully accept their spiritual power and to immediately pray for channels to put it to good use.

As a kind mentor once told me at a time when I did not understand the connection between my anger, my energy, and my experience of chronic crossed conditions at the time, "You need to take responsibility for the powers you brought into this life."

UNDERSTANDING INITIATORY CRISES

Many years ago, I received a call from a Christian woman in the South who wanted to know if her son had a curse placed on him by his girlfriend as he was bedridden in a hospital and doctors could not figure out what was wrong with him. The girlfriend sat by his bedside, holding his hand through the ordeal, but the only option left was to turn over every rock, and that meant turning to a practitioner in the spiritual arts.

My reading confirmed the allegiance of her son's girlfriend to him and that no curse had been placed. But other things were revealed as well, including the fact that this wasn't the first time that he'd found himself in a hospital without due medical cause. Most evident was that this was the work of something Divine — that there was a spiritual calling in this man's life that he had chosen to ignore time and time again. I'd never seen anything like it before, but when I asked the client if she understood what I was saying within the context of her 30-year-old son's life experiences, she responded affirmatively. There was a lifestyle that he'd been needing to put behind him, friends and enablers that he'd been warned he had to let go of, and he had refused. And now, time was running short.

Ultimately, the solution was a tea of Eyebright for wiping her son's eyelids and brow to help induce clarity, as well as a bedside visit from a pastor of her church whom she trusted would understand the calling on her son's life and encourage him to commit to involvement in the community under someone's guidance and mentorship.

Within a few years, it would be me who was experiencing spirit-led circumstances outside of what I considered to be humanly possible, urging me toward new ways of being and divinely-mandated responsibilities.

Across the world since time immemorial, certain individuals have experienced a holy terror under the guidance of Spirit. In *Rituals of Resistance,* Jason R. Young writes "the Kongolese often regarded illness as a spiritual summons such that a person afflicted with a particular disease might be initiated as an nganga [priest] specially suited to address that very sickness." Varying as widely in likeness and duration as do types of cultures that exist, the common thread connecting these ungrounding experiences is that they are, in actuality, a homecoming. For us to truly come home, however, we'll need help to strip away that which is false and to be granted new bodies and new vision.

Spiritual callings and initiatory crises can be scary and can seem to manifest as a sudden state of crossed conditions that cannot be remediated via spiritual cleansing or protection. Though divination by a trusted worker is of the utmost importance in discerning what is actually going on, the person in crisis, friends, or family members may notice signs like these:

- **Spirit visitations** from teaching or Helping Spirits.
- **Sudden visions** which are sometimes incapacitating.
- **Spontaneous possession** by spiritual entities.
- **Sudden physical illness** without known cause.
- **Sudden mental health crisis** or loss of sanity without known cause.
- **Sudden injury** resulting in intensified spiritual awareness.

It is likely that the person who is experiencing spiritual calling or crisis has had signs alluding to a spiritual destiny earlier in life, like the client's son mentioned earlier, or has been involved in the cultivation of spiritual gifts as an adult. These are helpful to consider when attempting discernment as to whether a spirit-led initiatory experience is actually taking place.

If you are someone who has found yourself in the midst of what you believe might be a spirit-led initiation or spiritual crisis:

- **Avoid desperation and victimhood.** Seek help if you feel despair.
- **Avoid delusions of grandeur.** You are probably not "the chosen one."
- **Pray for guidance and protection.** Call on God, your Ancestors, or Helping Spirits through prayer and simple rites to ground and center you.
- **Find support.** Tell affirming and uplifting family and friends about what you are going through and clearly state your fears, concerns, and needs. Spiritual crises can be confounding, not only threatening day-to-day life security, but also tearing away the very foundation of what you think it means to be a human with sovereign agency. Things will be lost. New gifts and opportunities will appear. Hold tight to nothing. Answering a calling means facing your fears and moving through them.
- **Find an affirming spiritual practitioner.** This person should be skilled in divination and preferably work within your own spiritual tradition or have the clarity and discernment to speak across cosmologies. Seek help when trying to divine the difference between a spiritual crisis and being cursed, crossed, or jinxed by an enemy.

UNDERSTANDING JINXES AND CROSSED CONDITIONS

One of the primary goals of hoodoo magical practice is to move through life free from hindrances to good health, financial security, peace of mind, emotional fulfillment, and general success. To find oneself thwarted in any of these arenas is to be jinxed or under crossed conditions.

The term jinx usually refers to your luck having been crossed up. If you were once a winner at bingo, the numbers no longer come out for you. If you had a gift for finding parking spaces, it has deserted you. Things break and can't be fixed. When you phone people, you either get a busy signal or you are put on hold. Most of all, you just can't win.

If a jinx persists to the point that your life is seriously messed up, you are said to be under crossed conditions. Invisible barriers block your path. Roads that once were open are closed. You lose your job, your car breaks down, and your health suffers. Your household may be affected.

Crossed conditions are not curses per se, but an enemy can curse you to suffer crossed conditions. And even if a curse is not the cause, you will certainly want to be uncrossed and free from jinxes.

Other factors that can cause crossed conditions range from demonic possession to intrusion by spirits of the dead upon one's person or home. Negative entities may have been directed to afflict you through a curse, or they may be wandering spirits who are parasitizing a human victim.

Most easily preventable are the crossed conditions that grow out of daily stresses, emotional wounds, and mental anxieties that have been left to fester unresolved. We shower and brush our teeth regularly, because we know that neglecting our physical hygiene will result in deterioration of our health, but neglecting our emotional, mental, and spiritual needs leads to our ruin as well.

There is something to be said for understanding that crossed conditions, especially in severe manifestations, have the potential to be initiatory. This is not the type of initiation that a priest or priestess in a religious tradition leads an adherent through, but the type that life itself is always presenting us. A time of financial destitution, the discovery of a lover's betrayal, or finding oneself the target of spiritual attack are all opportunities for us to see what we are made of — to gather our resources and put them to use toward self-preservation and personal growth. A near breakdown might mean that you are ripe for a real breakthrough. Even the evil deeds committed by others against you might lead you to discover the path of your highest calling.

UNDERSTANDING INTRUSIVE SPIRITS AND ENERGIES

Far more categories of spirits and conscious invisible energies exist than we are aware of and not all of them have our best interests in mind. Negative spirits range from the lost and confused to the outright malicious. Hoodoo practitioners recognize a number of paratisitcal or ill-intentioned spirits, from the Devil, demons, and tricksters to haints, ghosts, and the dead. Most are discarnate, but a special category, called hags, are actually living humans who take on spirit form at night to ride and drain the energy of their victims.

The dead not only include our revered Ancestors, but also unhappy and angry spirits. Those who died badly may be contracted by an enemy rootworker to ensure that curses are carried out, household or relationship discord is heightened, or that people are burdened down and confused. The unhappy dead may haunt homes or persons, and may be attached to objects as well; a felt sense for their presence can be cultivated by careful monitoring of one's mood and energetic field in different environments over time.

Negative spiritual intrusions can cause and exacerbate sorrow, manic behavior, depression, lethargy, and substance abuse. In some circles, spirits that bring about sadness are said to be low-vibration rate entities when compared to the likes of angels, who are seen as high-vibration rate entities.

To ensure alertness to the presence of spirit intrusions, magical attack, and the presence of harmful energies, it is important to understand one's personal "set point" in regards to mood and behavior. If you find yourself having seriously deviated away from how you normally feel day-to-day in a short amount of time — perhaps being less inclined to engage in activities that you usually find fulfilling — it is be wise to take a series of Uncrossing baths.

Divination can ascertain the presence of harmful entities, their origins, and the most effective means of removal. Traditional rootwork practices are quite effective in banishing intrusive spirits and providing protection against their return. Religious workers also affirm that most spirits can be commanded to leave in the name of Jesus Christ; some also work in the names of intercessors such as Archangel Michael, Archangel Raphael, and Saint Cyprian.

If dealing with negative spirits becomes too difficult for you to handle on your own, or if they return after a cleansing, do not hesitate to seek out the help of a qualified spiritworker. In my practice, where there is an intrusive energy, there is a wound that needs closing, so not only exorcism and protection are necessary — healing work of a strategic nature must follow.

UNDERSTANDING CURSES

Crossed conditions and even minor jinxes can be intentionally caused by an enemy who has laid tricks to mess you up. Crossed conditions that are the result of curses may drive you away from friends, or, if they are severe, they may lead you toward your grave. Generational and ancestral curses are known to have been wielded against whole families, households, and lineages in most world cultures. These are sometimes the root of chronic crossed conditions, resulting in clients who have always felt held back in life without a chance to pursue happiness unfettered by suffocating outside circumstances, or who have found that bad luck in health, money, and love follows a cyclical pattern.

The clearest way to discern the presence of an enemy attack is to find physical evidence of rootwork, such as powders laid down around your property or objects placed with malicious intent. Be particularly attentive to where you walk, for dusts or marks in your pathways and at thresholds may be evidence of foot-track work. Spiritual signs, such as warning messages delivered in dreams, and omens, such as the repeated discovery of dead animals in one's path, may also indicate that curses are being cast.

Many practitioners employ protective amulets, called apotropaic charms, which also provide warnings that evil is afoot. The best-known of these is a silver dime worn around the ankle or neck: if the dime blackens or the cord breaks it signals that harm is present; further divination will reveal its source so that the attack can be turned back. Another talisman worn on the body is the nazar (popularly called an "evil eye bead").

Guardian statues and figurines also provide protection from curses. If they fall over or break due to a magical attack, they are said to have "taken the hit" — but although the worst of the curse was diffused, further acts of reversing, cleansing, and protection are suggested.

Additional possible evidence of magical curses is to be found in the experience of physical illness such as sudden waves of exhaustion, headaches, a sensation of something crawling under one's skin or inside the body, or inexplicable weakness. In such cases, it is important to seek out a medical diagnosis to ensure that debilitation is not being caused by internal health conditions. If there is no physical evidence and medical tests come back clear, divination should be conducted, but it should be remembered that self-diagnosis through a reading can be misleading.

One of the primary reasons clients engage readers, seers, and diviners is to obtain a professional spiritual diagnosis in order to confirm or disprove a magical attack and provide techniques to dismantle it is, but it is important to beware those who prey on the vulnerable and uninformed. Once the diagnosis of a curse is made, there are stages of removal and protection. For the purposes of this book, we will treat or remediate curses with the same sorts of spells used for crossed conditions. Revenge spells and cursing spells to cast against those who have caused harm exist in abundance, but those are beyond the provenance of this book.

When a diagnosis reveals that a curse has been laid, it is wise to understand its severity, as some curses are easier to remove than others. Traditionally, it is believed that any curse that cannot be fouled and broken by destroying its physical elementsin fire or water is difficult to remediate. Likewise, curses laid in foreign lands or by practitioners who have since died are said to be difficult to resolve. Curses that involve the burying of dolls and effigies in graveyards are on the severe end of the spectrum, as are those that employ the aid of spirits of the dead in some capacity; the removal of these spirits through capture or exorcism often plays a role in successful remediation. The petitioning of gods and Nature Spirits to bring about the demise of a person or household is common. Curses that involve blood are perhaps the most harmful, but are fairly rare, regional, and found within specific religious or cultural groups. Any of these curses can be used to bring about total ruin and physical death.

Though it is a myth that curses only affect those who believe in them, paranoia and fear over a spiritual diagnosis certainly perpetuates them. Even when hiring an effective spiritual doctor to help remediate or resolve a curse, it is wise to ask for daily actions that are both cleansing and protective, or you can employ some of the simpler ones found within this book such as the reading of Psalms and performing bathing rites. These help you assert your agency and power in the face of your foes as well as give you something to focus on while expert aide works alongside you.

Our susceptibility to the effects of a curse goes beyond the employment of protective magic. True self-knowledge and self-mastery play a large role in our vulnerability and, like all crossed conditions, the experience of being cursed can lead us to resolve those internal matters that enabled it in the first place. Find the blessing in everything. The evil deeds committed by others may even lead you to discover the path of your highest calling.

INTERPRETING DREAMS, SIGNS, AND OMENS

The Dagara do not encounter a strange dream experience, and then wake up acting as if it had been a spectacle, a movie. Instead they take action. If you do not know what action to take, then you go find somebody who can help you find out. ... A lot of the times when you don't know what to do, you are advised to tell Spirit that you would like to do something, but you don't know what to do. This is considered acting on it. But it is not acting on it to think about it as some kind of interesting view. It is not supposed to be interesting, it is supposed to be effective.

— Malidoma Somé, Dagara Elder

Dreams are a way in which our Ancestors and guides bring us messages. They are useful in the work of self-mastery because the traps and tricks that our rational minds use to protect us from our fears and pain,are suspended while we dream. Dreams operate within the realm of Crazy Logic. The impossible occurs, and yet we find ourselves entirely invested in the narrative. They can bring warnings, visitations, and creative solutions. They can urge us to take new actions that our analytical minds had not considered.

Signs and omens are available to us in waking life all the time, but we do not always notice them or see them for what they are. They may appear coincidental, such as the repetition of the name of a person in our lives whom it is important for us to beware (or be aware) of, or encountering a particular concept or activity in rapid succession in multiple different environments, on peoples' lips, in books, and in song lyrics that all pertain to something that needs our attention or action.

We can ask for dreams, signs, and omens daily, and powerful questions we can pose before our Helping Spirits or a higher power include:

- **What is the true nature of this situation?**
- **Show me how / if making this decision serves my soul's purpose.**
- **What is the best next action for me to take regarding this situation?**
- **Show me a spell that I can perform to achieve this goal and the best next action for me to take after performing it.**
- **How am I getting in my own way?**
- **How am I lying to myself about this situation?**
- **How am I denying myself?**

TO RECEIVE A DREAM

To receive a meaningful dream about a situation or person of importance, pray for the dream before falling asleep. You may also write a question on a piece of paper and place it under your pillow or mattress before you go to sleep. Continue praying until you receive an answer.

TECHNIQUES FOR DREAM RECALL

Place a glass of water next to your bed with the intention that it will help protect your dreamstate by filtering out extraneous information and spiritual detritus. You may add a corner crumbled off of a Camphor square or a drop of Camphor essential oil to the glass. In the morning, pick the glass up, using your left hand, and toss it off your property (removing it is especially important if you are experiencing nightmares) or flush it down your toilet.

Alternatively, or in tandem, take a sip from a glass of water before going to sleep with the intention that you will remember your dreams upon waking. Place the water glass next to your bed or under it and, immediately upon waking, take another sip. This forms a bridge of consciousness through your dream state to your waking life.

HOW TO RECORD YOUR DREAMS

It is wise to keep a dream journal in which you record your sleep experiences, but we don't always remember the entirety of a dream upon waking, which can be a discouraging factor. To work around this, write your dreams down in first-person present-tense. Instead of writing "I saw a woman in a red dress," write "I am in a room with a woman in a red dress." Recording dreams and other trance states in this manner places us back in the midst of the experience, encouraging other aspects of it to come to light.

We may be tempted to ignore our dreams due to their seeming disconnection from our mundane lives, but a dream journal can help us to track the symbolic language with which our spirits speak to us. This can be one of the most effective ways of increasing our ability to interpret the language of spirits as the symbolic language of our dreams is often the same language they use with us in divination, meditation, and trance states.

If keeping a journal is too labour-intensive for you, and you sleep next to another, ask your bed-mate about his or her dreams every morning when you wake up. Regularly sharing dreams with another can also be a huge help in unpacking the full healing potential of our dreams.

HOW TO INTERPRET YOUR DREAMS

If, after recording you dreams, you have trouble interpreting them for the purpose of clarity and self-mastery, put them aside for a day or two. Then come back to what you wrote and, in a parallel column, begin recording lingering impressions — the most surface thoughts and feelings that arise from your remembrance, being as specific as possible. Were you afraid in the dream, or was it more of a suspicion? Did the person in the dream remind you of someone you used to know? How did you feel when you woke up?

Many dreams, like visions, are meant to lead to action. Ignoring them is both irresponsible and self-sabotaging. If you don't understand a dream or the actions to take based on one, pray for clarity and guidance until you do. Then, watch for signs, or additional dreams that follow. You may also choose to perform divination or ask someone to perform it for you.

DREAM BOOKS AS AN AID TO DREAM INTERPRETATION

Dream books are pamphlets that provide simple interpretations for dreams. Many of them also attach lucky betting numbers to dream images. Their use is an important part of the culture of conjure. To catch a lucky number in your dream, dab a handerkerchief with Aunt Sally's Lucky Dream Oil, roll it up, and sleep with it under your pillow. Look up your dream-image in the dream book and bet on the numbers that are provided.

ANISE PROMOTES DREAMS AND DIVINATION

Star Anise and Anise Seed aid in honing intuitive abilities. Put some into a little bag with Hops and Jasmine and place it beneath your pillow for restful sleep with predictive dreams. Float Anise Oil in water, shake it up, and spritz it around the bedroom to invite spirits in dreams. Anise Oil is also used to anoint one's temples, wrists, and hands before a divination. Anise incense can be used to smoke oneself, one's room, or one's divinatory tools.

PSYCHIC VISION MOJO HAND

In a white or red flannel bag, combine Star Anise, Anise Seed, Bay Leaf, Eyebright, Althæa Root, Solomon Seal Root, and Master Root along with your personal concerns and a petition for increased intuitive abilities. Feed the bag once per week with a Psychic Vision Oil, Aunt Sally's Lucky Dream Oil, or Florida Water. After the first week, keep it in a box on your altar or place it under your mattress for vivid dreams.

FORMAL METHODS OF DIVINATION AND READING

Divination is a tool for conscious engagement with otherwise undisclosed factors in life. It can be a first step toward understanding if you are crossed, jinxed, cursed, or merely having a bad day.

Gifted professional readers may employ divination to gain insight into a client's condition, foretell the future, determine which form of spiritual remediation is best in a given case, and estimate the likelihood for successful resolution to a problem. But just as home remedies are not neglected in lieu of an upcoming appointment with a medical professional, so should tools of divination exist in every home to provide clarity in times of need.

As a root doctor, there is a profound depth in the work I am able to do with clients who have their own form of divination to consult, have cultivated their own personal connection with the Spirit World, and are engaged with the signs that are making themselves known in their lives. This is not to imply that everyone should have the degree of connection a professional worker has, but it is everyone's birthright to have a basic connection to unseen guides.

It may take some experimentation before you find a form of divination right for you. Card reading is popular, but some folks are more attuned to scrying in crystal balls, coffee grounds, or tea leaves. Others take to augury, interpreting signs in nature, such as the flight of birds. From bone reading to geomancy to spirit boards, there is a tool of divination for everyone.

WATER FOR THE SPIRITS
I was taught to put a glass of water out before beginning a session to help filter messages brought forth and I find it to be a helpful conduit for inviting the wisdom, guidance, and clarity of my Helping Spirits into the process.

THREE CARDS DEALT OR CUT FOR A YES OR NO
Professor Porterfield of ProfessorPorterfield.com shares this simple card method that can be used to answer questions like "Am I cursed?"

Ask a clear yes or no question, shuffle the deck, and lay out three cards or cut the deck into three piles to get three cards. Interpret them as follows:
• **Three red cards:** A firm yes.
• **Two red cards and one black card:** A qualified yes.
• **Two black cards and one red card:** A qualified no.
• **Three black cards:** A firm no.

USING A PENDULUM TO REVEAL CROSSED CONDITIONS

Get a simple pendulum or suspend a ring on a thread. Tell it, "this is my *yes*" and swing it toward you and away. Tell it, "this is my *no*" and swing it side to side. Bring it to stillness. then ask, "Am I under crossed conditions?" You will get an answer. Further questions will reveal more detail.

7 TAROT CARDS THAT REVEAL CURSES ARE AFOOT

Conjureman Ali of HoodooPsychics.com tells us that if these cards show up in your tarot reading, you may have been crossed, hexed, or messed with:

- **The Tower:** Destructive magic has been worked to undermine your accomplishments. If you are married, someone is assaulting your marriage and the life you've built together. The curse will come upon you suddenly; everything will fall apart at once. This is swift and cruel magic.
- **10 of Swords:** Someone close to you has worked evil against you. This was an act of betrayal and treachery. When you least expect it they hit you where you are most vulnerable. This is harmful magic. Someone has a doll baby made on you and is sticking nasty pins in it.
- **5 of Swords:** A curse has been sent from afar. It is a spell to cause confusion and fights. It brings strife between you and another and overwhelms you with a pall of helplessness. The person doing this is taking delight in your suffering. Your enemy is a spiritual sadist.
- **8 of Swords:** You are bound and blindfolded in a curse of control and restriction. Someone wants you to stay put and to keep you under their thumb. They are doing their sorcery in a way that you cannot see, but it keeps you trapped and helpless. Time to call in some reinforcements!
- **The Devil:** Sorcery of the worst kind is seen in this card. It is dark magic with a mind all its own. Your enemy has unleashed evil forces, forces beyond their own control. A pact has been made and you are at the center of it all! Watch out for an unseen presence and supernatural disturbances.
- **5 of Cups:** This is the magic of mind and heart. Someone has cast a spell from a distance — across space and time — that keeps you locked in a spiral of sorrow and suffering. This spell originates from someone who is suffering and wounded. It is mean to affect family and relationships.
- **8 of Cups:** Magic is being used to drive you away from all that is good in your life. You will feel a sense of restless frustration. Someone has a spiritual prod and you are being prodded in a direction not of your choosing. This is magic that will send you away from home and hearth.

Uncrossing, 1925 - 2015. Art by Charles C. Dawson, Charles M. Quinlan, R.C. Adams, K. Rudin, Unknown Artist, Charlie Wylie, and cat yronwode for Famous Products, Oracle Products, R.C. Adams, Standard O & B Supply, and Lucky Mojo Curio Co.

Spiritual First-Aid Spells

Careful the tale you tell. That is the spell.
— Stephen Sondheim, "Into the Woods"

What are the stories that your life is founded upon? Stories of limitless freedom, eternal abundance, and that there is unconditional love for exactly the person you've come here to be? Look around you and you'll see a life that is at least partly the result of the stories you tell yourself about it.

At the root of every experience of bondage and limitation is a story. We often forget how the story got there in the first place. When we suddenly realize that we've been entertaining a harmful story for most of our lives, we might ask ourselves "Who put that there?" As children, we have stories imposed upon us all the time and, somewhere along the line, we may have made those stories our own.

Realizing that we've been living a story that does not serve us is half the battle. But after we realize it, how do we get ourselves out?

When performing magic to achieve a goal, we are launching a new story in which what we desire is true and present-tense. Allies in the botanical, mineral, and animal kingdoms can help, but the opportunity to change a story that you come across in your life — to let go of an old one and adopt a new one — is yours every moment of everyday. So go on...change a story and stick to the new one.

I find that my success rate when it comes to casting spells is much higher when I look to see if there is an underlying story behind what it is I feel I am lacking and commit to telling a new story about myself and about my life before gathering my spell materials. That Crown of Success working before going on a job interview sounds like a smart idea, but I also want to make sure that I'm telling myself a story in which I am worthy of my new pursuits and that, no matter what happens, I'm a lucky dog walking a blessed path. To live otherwise might be like spritzing myself with a nice-smelling cologne after not having showered for a week. I will have limited the impact of my intentions by having ignored their greater context. This is also an apt metaphor for why acts of uncrossing and spiritual cleansing are so important. Being disciplined about the stories we tell ourselves about our lives is an integral part of spiritual hygiene. We all have the power to change our lives via this act alone.

If you have experienced a minor jinx or temporary set-back, these four spiritual first aid techniques may be of help while you plan your spells. They will help you get through an emergency and will buy you some time as you prepare to do rootwork for jinx-breaking, uncrossing, and curse-removal.

LEAVE FEAR BEHIND

In the words of Frank Herbert, "fear is the mind-killer." It is debilitating to us, and, interestingly, it is rarely based in evidential truth. One of my favourite acronyms for fear is False Evidence Appearing Real. Many fears lurk within the shadows of our minds. Be vigilant regarding the tiny inner voices that tell falsely negative stories about who we are and what we can or cannot do. Becoming aware of them is half the battle against fear.

In difficult circumstances we may feel we have no option except to despair, but this is never truly the case. Every difficulty is an opportunity to make a decision about who we are choosing to be. Despair is the choice to ignore that opportunity and wrap ourselves up in chains instead.

This does not mean that you should not express fear, despair, or pain. Emotions are to be acknowledged, just as a healthy river is one that is always flowing. But it is also wise to remember that you are loved and, to quote the title of Rob Brezsny's book of wonders, *Pronoia is the Antidote for Paranoia: The Universe is Conspiring to Shower You with Blessings.* This is one of the best stories you can tell yourself, no matter where you are on life's journey.

PERFORM ACTS OF PRAYER AND FAITH

Prayer is communication with the Unseen. It is a conversation with Helping Spirits, Holy Powers, and that which we perceive as God. Acts of prayer and magic are assertions that we are co-creators of reality, and faithful prayer has been known to shake the foundations of Heaven and Earth. We can communicate with unseen powers at any time. To limit ourselves in this respect is to limit our potential for clarity and well-being.

Some magic spells contain a prayer or are intended to prayerfully be placed before a spirit who is humbly asked to intervene in human affairs, but other spells are an exertion of human will upon the Universe via subtle means. However, prayer and spells are not at odds, as we can pray to be led to a helpful healer or root doctor or pray to be shown an effective spell in our dreams. We can pray for signs and wisdom daily and receive them. To neglect prayer is to neglect an endless resource available to us at all times.

FEEL AND EXPRESS GRATITUDE

Entire books have been written on the power of gratitude and with good reason. Gratitude is one of the most powerful energies in the Universe. It is a state of being that is intimately connected with the energies of grace and flow. If we want to live a life of abundance and joy, we must choose again and again to live in a state of gratitude. Feel like you have little to be grateful for? Find something. Find something to be grateful for — the options are endless — and you immediately step into the flow of abundance. Gratitude shifts your perspective because it demands that we are in presence, not anxiously fearing the future or regretfully dwelling on the past. Choose to be disciplined about choosing gratitude and your life will change dramatically.

As practitioners of magic, gratitude is one of our best friends.

How do we assert that something we desire or intend is now true, simply because we've lit a candle or taken a magical bath? The way to assert that things are now the way we say is with gratitude. It is the perfect vehicle for manifestation because it is an embodied state of being that brings faith into the moment of NOW, for as Hebrews 11:1 says, faith is *"the substance of things unseen and the evidence of things hoped for,"*

Take a moment to be grateful for something. Go ahead. Perhaps for the fact that you can read the words on this page. Be with that for a moment and feel how your energy changes. Gratitude, for anything and everything, is a signal to Spirit and the great mechanism of which we are a part that we are willing and open to receive.

AFFIRM JOY AND PURPOSE

Few people can say that they live lives of joy, but most of us can point to a moment in which we've felt it.

Joy is intimately tied to purpose, and each of us has a purpose. When we talk about our dreams of writing a book, opening a restaurant, or teaching children to dance, we're talking about vehicles for our soul's purpose, whereas our purpose itself is an energy that we've come here to embody.

No two purposes are the same and living your soul's purpose as fully as possible is your responsibility. I experienced joy once at a dinner with fellow performance artists after a long day of rehearsing in a foreign country. It was fitting, as part of my soul's purpose is tied to community, travel, and the arts.

Discover your soul's purpose and find vehicles through which to manifest that purpose. This is the path to joy.

UNCROSSING AND SPIRITUAL CLEANSING

Uncrossing is undertaken to remove harmful energies, jinxes, curses, spirit intrusions, and self-imposed obstacles. Acts of uncrossing and spiritual cleansing are also performed at regular intervals by many practitioners as a form of energetic maintenance of self and of home.

Methods for uncrossing vary, but a good first step is to perform a divination to reveal who laid the trick that crossed you up. It may have come from far or near; the sender may be known or unknown. Divination should reveal both how the crossing came about and how to best remediate it.

Crossing spells can be worked at a distance with candles, dolls, or photographs, but often a known enemy is near. As Jim Haskins noted in *Voodoo and Hoodoo,* "since the principle of like-to-like is so commonly used, the source of the hurt often gives a clue to the placement of the hurting object. Thus headaches may be caused by something hidden in the pillow or under the head of the bed, impotence by something under the sheet or around the bed." In such cases, removal of the offending object is the priority.

After the divination, cleansing is undertaken. This will vary based on your situation. For instance, Chinese Wash is an excellent product for cleaning rooms and you can bathe with it as well, but if a foe has sprinkled bad luck powders for you to step in, a foot wash with Van Van, Fear Not to Walk Over Evil, and Blessing Bath Crystals might be more effective. Likewise, if your primary symptom is inability to find a job, you might try an Uncrossing bath followed by Block Buster, Road Opener, and Crown of Success work.

The duration of uncrossing treatments is variable: A person who is diligently sending in applications but still has trouble landing a position may find resolution after three baths with Van Van products, but if severe magical attack has been detected, baths may need to be undertaken daily for 21 days.

You may do the work yourself, but if divination indicates that you are beyond the help of do-it-yourself baths, you can hire a root doctor. Some readers suggest that clients find local workers for aid with hands-on baths and house cleaning, but others operate at a distance by performing proxy-work for clients. An authentic distance practitioner should send you baths and other supplies by mail, with instructions for use, or at least supply a shopping list of what you will need to get. This is called "backing up the work." A good root doctot will also not be upset if you consult another diviner for an occasional diagnostic "check reading" to see how things are going.

Some common herbs, roots, minerals, and zoological curios called upon for jinx removal, spiritual cleansing, and removing crossed conditions:

- **Agrimony:** Reverses a jinx or curse back to the one who sent it.
- **Alkanet Root:** Aids in the removal of money jinxes.
- **Ammonia:** Added in small amounts to cleansing baths and floor washes to "strip away" jinxes and crossed conditions.
- **Blueing:** Dissolved in water for bathing and cleansing floor washes.
- **Coffee:** Add a brewed cup to a bath for uncrossing or jinx removal.
- **Epsom Salts:** Removes negativity; good in "three-ingredient" baths.
- **Hyssop:** The preeminent purification herb in hoodoo, often called upon in conjunction with Psalms 51, which contains the verse *"Purge me with hyssop, and I shall be clean: wash me, and I shall be whiter than snow."* It is especialy ued for self-cleansing after performing harmful works.
- **Lemon Balm:** Removes love jinxes or crossed conditions in romance.
- **Lemon Grass:** A primary ingredient in Van Van products and Chinese Wash, used for removing crossed conditions and tricks laid by others.
- **Nettle:** Use it in jinx-breaking bath-teas; or combine it with other herbs and curios to sprinkle around the home.
- **Rue:** Popular in many magical traditions for breaking curses, hexes, and jinxes, and for removing effects of the evil eye.
- **Salt:** It is added to uncrossing, protection, and jinx-breaking baths.
- **Saltpeter:** Often found in simple "three-ingredient" cleansing baths and floor sprinkles.

Popular spiritual oils, incenses, baths, and powders used for jinx removal, spiritual cleansing, and removing crossed conditions:

- **13 Herb Bath:** A blend of 13 botanicals reputed to remove curses, hexes, jinxes, and crossed conditions. Often bathed in for 13 days.
- **Chinese Wash:** A liquid blend of Asiatic grasses and other ingredients used in spiritual cleansing floor washes.
- **Hindu Grass:** To clean out old messes and cut ties to past events.
- **Jinx Killer:** Used to break hexes, jinxes, and curses.
- **Run Devil Run:** Drives off demons, devils, and wicked people.
- **Uncrossing:** Used to remove crossed conditions and break jinxes.
- **Van Van:** Turns bad luck into good luck and opens roads.

HOW TO REVEAL AND BE RID OF YOUR HIDDEN ENEMY

To reveal a hidden enemy — whether a liar, gossiper, or wielder of magical attack who has crossed you up — take one of the Joker cards and the Two of Diamonds out of a deck of cards. With a sharp knife, slit the Two of Diamonds from diamond to diamond with a cut at least as long as the top of the Joker card. From the back of the Two of Diamonds, insert the Joker card vertically just inside the cut you've made and recite Matthew 10:26: *"Fear them not therefore: for there is nothing covered, that shall not be revealed; and hid, that shall not be known."* On the word "known," push the Joker halfway up through the cut to reveal the character on the card. Place both cards arranged in this fashion inside a Bible at Matthew 10:26. Look for signs over the next three days as to who the enemy is.

When your enemy has been revealed, open your Bible and take out your card arrangement. Using a Sharpie marker, write their name or the attributes that have been revealed above "The Joker" and slip the card out of the cut in the Two of Diamonds. Draw an X over each of the stars on the card while announcing the perpetrator's defeat. Fold the card once away from you and staple together each of the open edges. Write "You are bound up!" on both sides of the card and place beneath a candle dressed with Stop Gossip, Reversing, or Hot Foot Oil, or a mixture of these. Keep this Two of Diamonds for future spells of revealing that which is hidden.

HOW TO PERFORM A FOOTWASHING

Famously performed by Jesus on his apostles, ceremonial footwashing is a powerfully symbolic act of lovingkindness toward one's fellow human beings. In conjure, it is a form of cleansing and uncrossing, especially for clients who have been tricked through the feet. Self-application is rare but may be effective. It may also help in resolving ancestral crossed conditions.

Kneeling in front of your seated client with their legs exposed to the upper calf, place their feet in a basin of blessed and prayed over water. Using a bar of spiritual soap such as Florida Water, Sandalwood, or one containing cleaning herbs, wash the client's legs and feet while praying intently for renewal and for new roads to open in their life. Rinse them off and place their legs one at a time on a washcloth folded across your lap and dry them. Anoint the feet and legs with a blessing or drawing oil, stroking the calf muscles, and tug lightly on each toe. You may prophesy or provide intuitive insight. Hold both feet while saying a closing prayer and help the client to stand.

HOW TO PERFORM YOUR OWN UNCROSSING BATH

Many people break crossed conditions by the use of baths. In hoodoo, these are often performed by pouring water over one's head rather than sitting in a tub. It is traditional to rise before dawn and perform this work before speaking to anyone. Add a commercial preparation of Uncrossing Bath Crystals to about a gallon of hot water or steep an uncrossing herbal blend until the infusion begins to cool. When it is lukewarm, remove any large bits of herbal matter and take the pot to the bathroom. You may want to light a white candle on either side of the bathtub to create an entryway.

After your morning shower, turn off the water and pour your prepared bath over your head, or from the neck down. Place the now-empty pot between your legs to catch the run-off water. Using your hands, from head to toe, rub your body in a downward fashion. It is traditional to pray Psalms 51 or any other scriptural verse associated with spiritual cleanliness. You can also pray these words or similar ones with conviction: *"I am cleansed of any and all harmful energies that have attached themselves to me. I am uncrossed and made spiritually clean. Nothing can deter me from my blessed path."*

Affirm that you are made clean and new. These should be your first words of the day. When finished, carefully step out of the tub backwards through the threshold created by the two candles. Air dry.

Take the pot with the run-off water (even a small amount will do) to a crossroads where two roads intersect in a +. Toss the water over your left shoulder towards the West, stating *"I banish this condition and, as the sun sets in the West, so does it set upon my former condition."* Express gratitude to the spirit of the crossroads and walk home without looking back.

Alternatively, you may toss the run-off bath water at the base of a large tree that seems willing to drain this energy into the Earth. Traditional or not, I suggest offerings of Cornmeal or Tobacco be made to the tree for its help.

Remnant bath water is said to hold your former condition and personal essence. Some use it as an ingredient in house cleansing floor washes.

You may take uncrossing baths one time, or for three, seven, nine, or thirteen days, depending on the severity of the condition. When in the process of uncrossing and clearing, be mindful of your personal energy — who you allow into your home, who you shake hands with and come in contact with, old self-sabotaging thought patterns, and agreements you make. Be new.

Read more about uncrossing baths and floor washes in this book:
"Hoodoo Spiritual Baths" by Aura Laforest

HOW TO BAPTIZE A DOLL-BABY FOR UNCROSSING

Find a doll suitable to the gender expression of the person whom you will be working on, or sew one of cloth. Wax figural candles shaped like people work great. Load the doll with a petition paper wrapped around a strong personal concern such as a bit of hair. Add jinx-breaking botanicals and curios. If the doll is ceramic or porcelain, load it in a hole at the bottom and stop it with cork. In the instance of a wax figural candle, scrape out a bit of wax from the bottom and melt some back on over the loaded petition.

Baptize the doll by holding it in one hand and dipping the thumb of your opposite hand in a bit of whiskey and making the sign of the cross over the doll three times, stating *"I baptise this doll as N.N. in the name of the Father, the Son, and the Holy Ghost. It is no longer made of (materials used), but is now the body, flesh and blood of N.N., I hold your body in my hand and your fate in my grip."* Close your eyes and visualize traveling to the person in whose name you are baptizing the doll. Take a deep breath to bring some of them with you. Travel back to yourself and blow this into the doll's mouth. Viscerally feel the doll becoming flesh. You may have to do this more than once. Conclude by dipping your thumb in whiskey once more and repeating the phrases provided. The doll is now that person and what happens to it will happen to them. Tremendous care is advised. The words you speak over it and where you keep it all affect the person for whom it has been named.

To bring an end to a doll working, perform the rite of baptism with whiskey while stating firmly that the doll has returned to the materials from which it is made, and then dismantle it. You may burn it if you wish.

HOW TO UNCROSS A DOLL BY PROXY BATHING

Baptize a porcelain or wax doll-baby in the name of the person whom you are helping. While bathing, speak aloud how you are affecting them.

To remove crossed conditions, prepare a bath with an uncrossing herbal tea or add a drop of Uncrossing, Van Van, or Jinx Killer Oil to the water, pour the bath over the doll and brush it downward into another bowl that you will take down to the crossroads for disposal of the run-off toward the West.

For a drawing bath to instill positive conditions like money, love, luck, or mastery, use appropriate herbal teas or oils in water, pour the bath over the doll and brush it upward, then dispose of the run-off at a crossroads facing East.

When finished, wrap the doll in a white cloth, such as handkerchief, and place it somewhere safe until the next day.

UNCROSSING CANDLE SPELL

Take a white candle, either jumbo or glass-encased, and rub it down your own or your client's body while paying close attention to the top of the head, back of the neck, heart, stomach, back of the knees, and the soles of the feet. Visualize the candle picking up any and all harmful energies. Light the candle without dressing or fixing it and let it burn down completely.

UNCROSSING SUGAR BATH

The following four-ingredient, five-day uncrossing bath comes, via Harry Hyatt's five-volume *Hoodoo-Conjure-Witchcraft-Rootwork* collection, from Informant 1532, a professional root doctor of Memphis, Tennessee. Hyatt interviewed her in October, 1938, and the transcription includes Hyatt's questions as well. It was provided to me by Deacon Millett of Four Altars Church in his book *Hoodoo Honey and Sugar Spells.* He calls it "an excellent example of down-home simplicity in Southern conjure," Here it is, verbatim:

"There's another bath that I bathe. I'm telling you to take five baths in this, for five days. Now, this bath that I fix — now my best ingredient in this bath is soda [baking soda, sodium bicarbonate, a natural anti-bacterial deodourant]. And into this two tablespoons of soda I add two tablespoons of sugar, two of salt, and two of mustard powder, and that's all. Then you place this mixture in a small quantity of water, about four cups of water, let it be real warm, and then you take that and sponge your whole entire body with it, and then you rinse it off."

("In all this bathing, according to your motions, you always bathe down?")

"Down, down, like you say. If you bathe yourself down, that sugar will sweeten your body. The salt is a saving ingredient, isn't it? That mustard is for sweating possession out of you, and that soda opens the pores and dries that stuff out. And regardless of whatever may be done, whatever, you'll sure be able to come free."

("You take this bath if anybody has put a spell on you and this bath draws it out?")

"It really will, yeah, it really will. And then it'll drive enemies away and make peace in the time of confusion. Then it'll help you to be successful, to go forth into the world and accomplish what you try to accomplish. You'll find there's nothing under the sun no greater than those four little common things."

COFFEE UNCROSSING BATH
Dilute 1 strong cup of coffee, a capful of Ammonia, and an infusion of Rue in a gallon of water as a strong uncrossing bath that also removes the effects of the evil eye, and alleviates spiritual lethargy or depression.

SPIRITUAL CLEANSING BATH WITH COLOGNE AND SALT
Add a splash of Florida Water Cologne and a handful of Sea Salt to a Hyssop infusion and bath in the manner of an Uncrossing bath. You can also add Ammonia (heavily diluted) to increase the strength of this bath.

APPLE CIDER VINEGAR AND SALT BATH
Add 1 cup of Apple Cider Vinegar and a ½ cup of Salt to a full tub of bath water. Soak for at least 10 minutes and be sure to douse every part of your body, head included.

DR. E.'S OKRA BATH TO REMOVE CROSSED CONDITIONS
To remove serious crossed conditions, crush thirteen Okra pods in a large pot of warm water, using your hands to break them apart as much as possible. Use a strainer to remove the large bits vegetable material so that you are left with a mixture of water and the slippery mucus for which the plant is known. Bathe downward in the standard manner of an uncrossing bath but rinse yourself off afterwards.

"3-INGREDIENT" BATH OR SPRINKLE TO REMOVE EVIL
(from Hoodoo Herb and Root Magic by catherine yronwode)
Ingredients vary, but one popular "three-ingredient" purification bath combination uses a teaspoonful of Saltpeter, a half-cup of Salt, and a tablespoonful of powdered Blueing in a bath; another formula substitutes a half-cup of Epsom Salts for the Blueing. When taking such a bath, wash downward only, to remove all evil influences. The same mixtures can be used as dry granules to sprinkle around the house for spiritual cleansing.

PURIFYING BURDOCK SCRUB FOR HOME OR BUSINESS
(from Hoodoo Herb and Root Magic by catherine yronwode)
Burdock is a cleansing, uncrossing, and protective herb. Brew the root into a tea with Broom Corn, Rosemary, or Lemon Grass, strain it, and add it to scrub water to purify the premises.

AURA LAFOREST'S JINX KILLER FOOT BATH

Add 1 teaspoon ground Black Pepper to a packet of Jinx Killer Bath Crystals. Use in foot baths to take off tricks you may have stepped over.

HOW TO PERFORM AN EGG CLEANSING

The use of a hen's egg to cleanse a client and remove harmful energies is found in magical traditions worldwide, and though popularly known through Latin American curanderismo limpia practices, egg cleansing and uncrossing (especially with an egg from a black hen) is found in hoodoo as well. It is a favoured method for removing the evil eye, an unintentional curse placed by a jealous person. It can also help remove energetic intrusions and parasites.

To start, take a clean, raw, room-temperature egg, or one anointed with Uncrossing oil, and ask it to absorb any evil conditions within or around the client. Roll the egg downward along your client's body or aura while praying fervently that they be cleansed of any and all things that are not in alignment with their highest good. Visualize darkness entering the egg from the client's body and energy, and continue until the egg feels full. Dispose of the egg by breaking it at a crossroads or the base of a strong tree, throwing it into a river, or cracking it into a glass of water to read for signs (and then disposing of it). Dress the client with Blessing, Drawing, or Attraction Oil to finish.

PROFESSOR PORTERFIELD'S SEVENS TO BREAK A JINX

You can use this ritual to help kill or break off a jinx that has been thrown on you. For this work you will need the 7 of Spades from a used deck of cards and the 7 of Diamonds from a new deck of cards. Take an X-Acto knife and carefully cut the seven Diamonds out of the 7 of Diamonds card and put them away in safe place. Dress the corners of the 7 of Spades with Jinx Killer Oil, place it before a white 7-knob candle, and pray the 91st Psalm over them.

On the first day of the ritual, as the hands of the clock are falling, dress the candle with Jinx Killer Oil, and light it. As the first knob burns use a pink eraser, or a piece of sandpaper, to erase the center Spade from the card completely. Glue one of the cut out Diamonds onto the space where the Spade was. Let the first knob burn down and snuff out the candle. On the following six days repeat the actions of the first day until the card is empty of spades and full of Diamonds. Dress the card with Attraction Oil and keep it in a safe place or on your altar.

SECRET UNCROSSING TRICKS ON FAMILY MEMBERS

The laying of tricks can be done with beneficial intent. Chinese Wash, or condition oils such as Uncrossing, Van Van, and Jinx Killer, can be added to the liquid bodywash and shampoo containers of loved ones, and folks have long fixed family members' clothing with intention by adding condition bath crystals to laundry rinse cycles. You are encouraged to use your imagination.

HOW TO PERFORM A CLEANSING FLOOR WASH

It is traditional to perform this work before dawn and before speaking to anyone. Make sure the space is physically clean before beginning.

Add a tablespoon of Chinese Wash to a bucket of hot water. Alternatively, add Van Van Bath Crystals or an infusion of Lemon Grass to soapy or plain water. Other cleansing herbs may be included, and if an uncrossing bath has been performed, some leftover bath water can be added as well. Pray over this that all harmful energies in the space be removed. With a mop, squeegee, or sponge, clean from the back room to the front room. If the space is multi-floored, start with the top floor and work your way down. In carpeted rooms, lightly wet a broom and sweep it over the carpet. Give the entryways extra attention. Use a white cloth to wipe down surfaces such as windowsills. As you cleanse, pray that your space is made clean and new; Psalms 23 is traditional. Some folks move a cross-shaped figural candle dressed with Blessing Oil from room to room after each is cleansed. When finished, pour the leftover scrub water into your front yard or dispose of it at a crossroads.

Next, make a new floor wash using a few drops of condition oil or herbs such as Basil for protection, Mint for money, or Rose for love. Mop or scrub from the sidewalk or entryway toward the door. You need not take this "drawing" floor wash into the actual home. Pour the remnant wash in your backyard or, if living in an apartment, down your toilet. Anoint all doors and windows leading to the outside world with Fiery Wall of Protection Oil in a five-spot pattern — a dab in each corner and one in the center.

HOW TO UNJINX A HOME WITH INCENSE

When enemy tricks have been laid in the home or on clothing and cannot be located for removal, close all windows and doors to the outside and burn Jinx Killer Incense in each room with all drawers, closet doors, and cabinets kept open. When the home has been thoroughly smoked, open the windows to carry away the jinx and finish off with Blessing and Protection work.

HOW ROOT DOCTORS UNCROSS DISTANT CLIENTS

If you live far away far away from your root doctor, he or she may prescribe cleansing supplies from a reputable order house or make supplies and mail them. Uncrossing and 13 Herb Baths are the foremost tools in the root doctor's first aid kit; in addition to these, as the old ads tell us, the most common prescriptions are to "wash away that unclean condition" and "clear away that evil mess" with Chinese Wash, and to use Van Van Oil to "drive away evil spirits."

If bathing is not practical due to physical inability or privacy concerns, root doctors may do the work for clients at their own altars by lighting Uncrossing candles set atop petition papers; burning, scattering or burying objects related to the crossed conditions; or through the proxy-bathing of dolls after they have been loaded with the client's personal concerns, baptised, and brought to life as stand-ins for the clients themselves.

AFTER THE UNCROSSING: BLESSING AND PROTECTION

According the physics concept of plenism attributed to Aristotle, nature abhors a vacuum. When energy is intentionally banished or removed, the space it occupied should just as intentionally be filled with something new, lest after all of our careful cleansing we leave what fills us back up to happenstance. In other words, upon completing an uncrossing bath, works of blessing, drawing, or protection should follow. To do this, pray a prayer of blessing, such as the 23rd Psalm, over yourself from foot to head, going upward. Then speak an affirmation and anoint your pulse points with a condition oil such as Protection, Crown of Success, Money Drawing, or High John the Conqueror to cultivate what you desire. You may also dust yourself with a suitable sachet powder in an upward manner. If you have no specific needs for protection or drawing, use Blessing or Tranquility products.

If you are using Fiery Wall of Protection Oil, you could affirm: *"I am protected from any and all harm. I dress myself in the armour of God and no weapon formed against me shall prosper."*

If you are using Money Drawing Bath Crystals, you could affirm, *"The abundance of Nature showers blessings upon the earth. The Lord God pours down for me a blessing until there is no more need."* Contemplate the goodness of the land, and the storehouse of abundance set forth before you.

Take a moment to bask in the glow of your affirmation. Experience it as already true and be grateful for what has been achieved.

UNCROSSING MONEY: DELIVERANCE FROM POVERTY

Spiritual work to attract luck, money, and worldly success is called "helping yourself" and the quest for financial stability is one of the primary reasons that people seek out root doctors and practitioners. Conversely, the lack of a stable income leads many to question whether or not something is "holding them back" or whether their money has been crossed or cut off.

Though thousands of spells, techniques, and tricks for attracting money exist, it is only by first discerning and then remediating the actual root cause of financial distress that success in these realms can be achieved. A one-time money spell is rarely the answer to chronic financial difficulty, but coupling remediation of the basic concern with optimization of mundane real-world efforts can often produce concrete results in a relatively short amount of time.

Some of the signs of crossed or jinxed money include inability to find a job, inability to get repayment of debts owed, repeated thefts of money or goods, and the chronic unexpected breakage of durable expensive goods just as their warranties expire, requiring complete and costly replacement.

Aside from jinxes, our own beliefs about money may hold us back. The belief that Spirit is separate from Matter is a frequent obstacle to financial success. When we use the information, wisdom, and opportunities that our guides and Helping Spirits provide for us and take decisive action toward our goals, the response of the world illustrates how these realms are intertwined.

Additionally, some of us struggle with the pervasive belief that one should not ask for what one wants, but only for what one needs. This is a sure way to ensure that one remains limited in experience and pleasure in this world. Spiritual baths for increasing a sense of self-worth are optimal in these cases.

It may also be necessary to examine self-limiting fears and beliefs around worth, prosperity, and success in one's ancestral line to see if negative belief patterns exist on a family level. Ancestral concerns are prevalent in the descendants of those who were economically exploited or immigrants whose struggle for survival came at the cost of their personal dreams. In these cases, seeking out a worker who is adept in ancestral clearing work is suggested.

Money and success are spirits themselves, and in the words of Jason Miller, author of *Financial Sorcery,* "If you want money to work for you, you need to learn about it, just as you would a spirit. Spirits have specific likes and dislikes, and so does money." Honour, movement, and charity are a few of the qualities he lists as associated with the spirit of money.

Some common herbs, roots, minerals, and zoological curios called upon to banish crossed money conditions and to restore prosperity:

- **Alfalfa:** For protection from poverty by helping to ensure basic needs.
- **Alkanet Root:** For protecting money and helping to build a savings.
- **Alligator Foot:** For luck in games of chance and holding onto money.
- **Bayberry Root:** For attracting money through luck.
- **Bay Laurel:** For mental clarity, success, and victory in all matters.
- **Calamus Root:** For granting control over persons and situations.
- **Cinnamon:** For attracting money and that which is desired.
- **Five Finger Grass:** For skill and to ensure that favours are granted.
- **Gravel Root:** For attracting employment and getting hired by others.
- **High John the Conqueror Root:** For attracting money and success.
- **Irish Moss:** For attracting money and saving money in business affairs.
- **Licorice Root:** For granting control over persons and situations.
- **Lodestones:** Magnetic iron ore trained to attract that which is desired.
- **Pyrite (Fool's Gold):** A mineral for attracting money and success.
- **Sampson Snake Root:** Attracts respect from peers and authority.
- **Sassafras**: For business and turning money into wealth. Add to wallet.
- **Solomon Seal Root:** For financial success grounded in wisdom.
- **Mercury Dime:** For financial luck, especially if minted in a leap year.
- **Thyme:** For helping money grow. Sprinkle a bit in your wallet.

Popular spiritual oils, incenses, baths, and powders used for removing money troubles and bringing in financial luck, money, and success:

- **Attraction:** For attracting love, money, or something more specific.
- **Cleo May:** For attracting generous lovers; helpful for sex workers.
- **Crown of Success:** For attracting respect and helping ensure victory.
- **Fast Luck:** A New Orleans formula for attracting love or money fast.
- **Good Luck:** An all-purpose formula for luck in love and money.
- **Hoyt's Cologne:** Used in both spiritual and financial matters.
- **Money Drawing:** For attracting money to oneself or to a business.
- **Money Stay With Me:** For helping one to save more than is spent.
- **Road Opening:** For clearing the way and attracting new opportunities.
- **Special Oil #20:** An all-purpose formula used for all good works.
- **Steady Work:** For getting hired for a 9-to-5 or any other type of gig.

BATH TO BREAK A MONEY JINX
Perform an money-uncrossing bath on yourself using an infusion of Lemon Grass, Sassafras, and a small amount of Alkanet Root (a natural red dye). Do this for three days.

DOUBLE ACTION CANDLE TO KILL A MONEY JINX
Butt a double-action green and black candle of any size by chopping off the wick end on the green side and carving a new point on the black side. Run the candle through your auric field in a downward manner, visualizing it picking up any energies contributing to blockage in your financial life. If you have a known enemy, dress it with Reversing Oil; otherwise use Van Van Oil to change your luck. Put it in a candle stand and light it. While it burns, anoint your wallet, purse, and all bank cards with Jinx Killer or Uncrossing Oil.

UNCROSSING A JINXED PLACE OF BUSINESS
If your place of business seems crossed or jinxed and money is not coming in, you will want to cleanse it. You can do a complete floor washing, like the one described in this book, but if the place you are cleaning is easier to sweep or vacuum than to mop, then simply get a packet of Nettle herb, a packet of Agrimony herb, and a half-handful of salt, and mix them together while praying the 23rd Psalm. Sprinkle and scatter this dry mix all over the floor, let it stay over night, and sweep or vacuum it all up early the next morning. Dispose of the used herb mix off the property. Follow with a business-drawing floor wash.

BUSINESS DRAWING FLOOR WASH
After you have cleansed a place of business, it's time to draw in customers and money. On a Friday morning, before speaking to anyone, add a few drops of your first urine of the day, three tablesoons of Chinese Wash, and nine drops of Money Drawing Oil to a bucket of scrub water. Mop the door area inward.

HEAL AND IMPROVE HOME FINANCES BATH BLEND
(from "Hoodoo Spiritual Baths" by Aura Laforest)
Boil up a pot of water and add Fenugreek Seed, Irish Moss, Alfalfa, Mallow (Althaea) root, and salt. Add to the bath weekly or use a quarter cup of the tea in the wash water for the house every week. Dispose of the remains over the side-walk leading to the home.

FINANCIAL UNCROSSING BATH
(from "Hoodoo Spiritual Baths" by Aura Laforest)
Combine Pine Needles, Basil, and Sage for use as a bath or floor wash. This combination will uncross and cleanse away financial poverty and negativity, draw in money abundantly, and help you to spend it wisely.

CONJUREMAN ALI'S MONEY JAR TO PROTECT MONEY
At ravenconjure.blogspot.com, ConjureMan Ali says, "Money is a fluid concept and also very susceptible to being jinxed. In fact, when I come across people who have been the victim of a curse or even the evil eye, I find that their finances are the first thing to go." Here is his advice for remediation:

"Write your petition directly onto a $20.00 bill, asking for money to come to you, enough to cover your expenses and help you live comfortably, and for the money to stay with you. Cover and cross this petition with your name by turning it clockwise ¼ of a turn and writing your name three times over it. Five-spot the bill with a money oil and place a magnet in the center with Cinnamon, Five Finger Grass, Bayberry, Blue Flag Root, and either Alfalfa, Alkanet, or Devil's Shoe Strings. Fold the bill toward you, turn it clockwise and fold it again until you have a little packet. Put the packet into a jar of Sugar and breathe Psalms 23 into the jar before you shut it close. Place the jar on a prosperity altar, light candles on it, shake it up and pray over it. It will sweeten and draw money to you, but it will also protect your money from jinxes, mishaps, and other things that cause money to slip out of your hands.

"Keeping a bowl of Alfalfa in one's kitchen or sprinkling it in the four corners of the room is aanother helpful old-time conjure trick for keeping poverty at bay.

"Employing money protection tricks and Money Stay With Me supplies can open the door to serendipitous experiences both seemingly mundane and fantastical. Sales and deals can show up at the most fortuitous moments and things that would end up getting lost or breaking and needing to be replaced have more staying power, helping you to curb financial outflow."

A LUCKY COIN FROM AN ANCESTRAL LAND
If your Ancestors came to America under duress and the family is now poor, acquire an antique coin from the ancestral land as a token of "what once was and may yet be." Carry it as a prosperity talisman to enlist ancestral aid in regaining the family's wealth and status that was lost in the diaspora.

UNCROSSING "TAINTED" MONEY IN YOUR WALLET

If you have received money from a bad source, you have two choices: give it all to charity or take the taint off of it. An old-fashioned way to cleanse paper money is to put in your wallet with dried whole mint leaves. Write out Deuteronomy 8:18 (*"Remember the Lord thy God: for it is he that giveth thee power to get wealth"*) on one of the bills, and give that one to a beggar.

STRONG MONEY-HOLDING MOJO HAND

(from Hoodoo Herb and Root Magic by catherine yronwode)

Jam a Silver Dime into an Alligator Foot so that it looks like the 'gator is grabbing the coin. Wrap it tightly with three windings around of red flannel, sprinkling Sassafras root chips between each layer as you wind, and sew it tight. Just as the Alligator Foot holds the coin and won't let go, so will you be able to save instead of spend.

KAST EXCELSIOR'S TRIPLE STACKED MONEY SPELL

This is called "Jupiter's Triple-Stacked Money Condition Petition Spell" because it calls in and "stacks" three distinct conditions in sequence to manifest a specific set of experiences in the life of the spell's target.

Start with the 4th Pentacle of Jupiter from *The Key of Solomon*. It should be about four inches in diameter. You can print or scan a copy out so that it fits on about a quarter-page of a standard letter-size paper, or, if you like, you can draw it yourself by copying an example in a book or online.

On the blank backside of the pentacle, write in an unbroken cursive script around the outer edge: "With opened road the money flows into my hands it grows and grows." Then write the target's name (plus optional business name, bank, or investment account numbers) in the center. Anoint the outer edge of the circle with Road Opener Oil, an inner circle with Money Drawing Oil, and the center point with Money Stay With Me Oil or Prosperity Oil.

The charm is then smoked with the corresponding incenses and folded into a mojo bag or set beneath dressed and fixed glass-encased vigil candles.

TO TAKE OFF A MONEY-JINX WITH CHAMOMILE

(from "Hoodoo Herb and Root Magic" by catherine yronwode)

Carry Chamomile in a mojo bag with Alkanet and one other uncrossing herb, such as Lemon Grass, Rue, or Agrimony. There should be three kinds of herbs in the bag, plus three coins.

USING POWDERS AND OILS TO GAIN EMPLOYMENT

To help ensure that your resume stands out from competing applicants, dust paper applications with Van Van powder to remove crossed conditions, plus Steady Work, Crown of Success, and Look Me Over powders for success. If applying for jobs online, anoint yourself and the corners and center of your computer keyboard with these condition oils each day before sitting down to begin your work of applying. This technique is also applicable for artists and freelancers seeking gigs. Dress yourself and your clothing with oils, powders, or baths before going to your interview!

ELIMINATING DEBT

The late Dr. E. of ConjureDoctor.com wrote a blog post in 2011 regarding debt, how collections agencies work, and how to unbury oneself via both magical and legal means from the repercussions of this modern day form of economic enslavement. It begins with understanding and demanding debt validation to stop harassing phone calls, which also requires that collections agencies provide documentation proving your debt, which they most likely do not have or will not be able to show in a timely manner. It is a worthwhile read that you can find online at: conjuredoctor.blogspot.com/2011/11/hoodoo-spell-eliminate-your-debt.html

MONEY STAY WITH ME WORK TO REMAIN DEBT-FREE

Budgeting and financial planning are well supplemented by Money Stay With Me Work, the essence of which is the motto of Lucky Mojo Curio Company's product line of the same name — "It's not how much you get, it's how much you can hold on to!" One of the oldest tricks of this kind is to place a lodestone dressed with Money Stay With Me Oil and Magnetic Sand on your nightstand, bureau, or chest of drawers. Money kept under the stone for seven days can be spent on what you need and will never go to waste.

WORKING WITH LODESTONES FOR PROSPERITY

Lodestones can be used to attract anything you desire. To work with one for money, wash it in whiskey or Hoyt's Cologne and baptise it in the name of the Father, Son, and the Holy Ghost while giving it a name and telling it what it will be used for. Dress it with money oils and place it on top of a petition for financial abundance. Feed it daily by sprinkling Magnetic Sand on it and telling it that as it is fed, so does it bring to you that which you desire.

UNCROSSING LOVE: DELIVERANCE FROM LONELINESS

Crossed conditions can affect the love life with bad luck. Divination may be undertaken to ascertain the cause, but in cases of spiritual love troubles, unlike general crossed conditions, sufferers are often able to either accurately name the person who messed them up, or, if they are honestly self-searching, they will know that they somehow did it to themselves.

Love-crossings may be suspected when people who are of normal sociability cannot find true love, get dates, or even hook up for casual sex, no matter how long they search. Crossed conditions may also be a factor in the lives of those who are repeatedly lonely because "love doesn't last," those who can find a date but never a fiance, or who can become engaged but are never married. These lovelorn ones may be doing everything right, but picking the wrong people to love or they may be dealing with deflected issues of self-esteeem and self-love; however, there are other reasons people become crossed-up in love, and not all of them are the result of self-wounding or poor life choices. People may, in fact, be love-cursed.

Curses on love include blockages placed on a person by a jealous love-rival, roots thrown by an ex-lover or ex-spouse who is seeking revenge, love-binding or tied nature spells performed by a possessive lover, and life-draining impediments placed on young people by negative or needy family members who wish to forbid their victims from marrying and leaving home.

Generational love curses are another type of love-crossing. These quite often arise due to someone's anger over a broken engement or a child borm out of wedlock decades ago. Familial curses of this type may be recognized by such signs as all of the males in the family dying young, or all of the women being able to have children, but not able to marry or hold a man.

Finally, there are people who simply cross up their own love lives. Some do this by succumbing to obsessive sorrow over a break-up or divorce, which leaves them open to negativity and stress. Others get into trouble by calling upon unclean or intranquil spirits to mess up ex-lovers or to force a reconciliation. Wicked spirits do not always do the job they were called up for; instead they may become attached to those who summon them and feed upon their sorrow. Situations like this are best treated as cases of spirit intrusion.

In the face of all these issues, love uncrossing is supportive and affrmative work, and it can be very rewarding, because it is the first step on the path to finding new love.

Some common herbs, roots, minerals, and zoological curios called upon to end crossed love conditions and to restore pleasure and romance:

- **Bay Leaf:** Grants calm wisdom to see a way forward.
- **Broom Straws:** To sweep away crossed conditions at the doorway.
- **Burdock Root:** Used to revive male nature if it has been crossed.
- **Calamus Root:** To unjinx sexual nature if it has been tied.
- **Dill:** An herb that beaks jinxes and crossed conditions in love.
- **Hyssop:** For forgiveness of sin if the crossed conditions were the result of one's own unworthy actions, bad temper, cheating, or wrong-doing.
- **Lemon:** To cut away old love ties and clear the way for new love.
- **Lemon Balm:** Added to baths and candle rites to remove love jinxes.
- **Lemon Verbena:** It cuts unhealthy ties to lost love or love gone wrong.
- **Master Root:** Helpful in cultivating self-control and self-mastery.
- **Mint:** To break jinxes in the home; to protect that which is closest to you.
- **Orange:** A symbol of marriage, it is also a powerful cleanser.
- **Rosemary:** Empowers the feminine. Promotes positive family relations.
- **Rose:** Returns romance, love, and pleasure to the senses.
- **Rue:** A member of the Orange and Lemon family, it clears off evil.
- **Self Heal (All Heal):** Promotes health in all areas of life.
- **Solomon Seal Root:** Enhances wisdom, breaks patterns of victimhood.
- **Queen Elizabeth Root:** For the strength and power of women.
- **Violet:** The heart-shaped leaves ease heart-break and bring in love.
- **Walnuts:** Used in a bath to break unwanted or obsessive love.

Popular spiritual oils, incenses, baths, and powders used for removing crossed conditions in love, romance, or sexual nature:

- **Attraction:** For attracting love, money, or something more specific.
- **Clarity:** To clearly see the true nature of a relationship or a partner.
- **Cut and Clear:** To remove love obsessions or fixations on the past.
- **Jinx Killer:** Used to break hexes, jinxes, and curses of all kinds.
- **Look Me Over:** To attract friendship, romance, and potential love.
- **Love Me:** To draw love by making oneself loving and loveable.
- **Nature:** To restore sexual energy after a break-up or having been tied.
- **Tranquility:** For centered calmness while awaiting new love.
- **Uncrossing:** Used to remove crossed conditions and break jinxes.

TO BREAK A LOVE JINX WITH A BATH

If you believe your love life has been jinxed either by an enemy or for other reasons, bathe in a tea of Dill, Lemon Verbena, and Rue for nine days.

TO BREAK A LOVE JINX WITH A CANDLE

To remove a jinx on an existing relationship, write a petition paper using the names of both parties crossed by the word "UNJINXED" and anoint the four corners and the center with either Jinx Killer or Reversing Oil (use the latter if a known third-party has placed the jinx). Butt a red and black jumbo double-action candle, and with a pin write *"All hexes, jinxes, and curses are removed from this relationship"* on the black part of the candle backwards (in mirror-writing) from the wick end to the center. Write *"Love and peace have been restored to this relationship"* on the red part of the candle from the wick end to the center, writing normally. Starting at the center of the candle, stroke oil onto the candle, away from you on the black part with the wick facing away and then toward you on the red part with the wick facing you. Melt the bottom of the candle so it stands firmly in a candleholder and place it on a heatproof dish with Dill, Lemon Verbena, and Rue sprinkled around it.

TO RESTORE NATURE WITH DILL AND GINGER

(from Hoodoo Herb and Root Magic by catherine yronwode)

Make a tea with Dill leaf and Ginger root, strain out the herbs, rub this tea over your body, and let it dry. Do this for nine days, making a new batch of tea each day. This is deemed to be especially helpful for a person whose nature (sexual vitality) has been hoodooed or taken away.

TO UNJINX SEXUAL NATURE WITH CALAMUS

(from Hoodoo Herb and Root Magic by catherine yronwode)

Boil chopped-up Calamus roots in a quart of whiskey until the liquid is reduced to one pint. Strain out the roots and add a fresh pint of whiskey. Drink a small spoon-sized dose daily as a medicine to restore stolen or jinxed nature.

TO REVIVE MALE NATURE WITH BURDOCK

(from Hoodoo Herb and Root Magic by catherine yronwode)

If someone fixes a man's sex life, he can steep a whole Burdock root in Olive Oil and use the oil as a genital rub to restore his power.

DR. E.'S LOVE UNCROSSING RITUAL

Dr. E. of ConjureDoctor.com fashioned a formula and spellwork that he called "Love Uncrossing," the aim of which is to drain the emotional charge from past relationship pains away and, at the same time, invite the energy of love to restore your sense of lovability and self-worth. In my own experience, work in this regard need not take place only in the aftermath of a failed romance, but in any situation in which we've come to see that the heart needs healing. Love Uncrossing work can re-align a person with Love, their capacity to love and be in the flow of love and connection with themselves and others. The series of soaking baths he gave instructions for on his blog can be performed if you find yourself stuck in an emotional pattern, or as a healing retreat to perform at least once per year. Read more online at: ConjureDoctor.Blogspot.com/2009/08/getting-past-break-up-of-love-or.html

BATH FOR SELF-LOVE AND TO RID ONESELF OF SHAME

Beginning on a Monday during the waning moon, bathe in an infusion of Hyssop, Lavender, and Rose, asking them help you let go of self-judgment. Rub your body downward while praying Psalms 51. Dispose of the run-off water at a crossroads, dispersing any shame you are carrying to the four corners of the Earth. Dress your body in an upward manner with Blessing and John the Conqueror Oils while praying Psalms 139:14, which reads *"I will praise thee; for I am fearfully and wonderfully made: marvelous are thy works; and that my soul knoweth right well."* Perform the rite for seven days.

CUT AND CLEAR WORK AFTER LOVE IS GONE

To cut and clear is to sever emotional ties with a person in whom you've invested too much of yourself, such as an unrequited love or a past partner whose memory you've yet to release. Cutting and clearing brings resolution to unwanted emotional patterns. Whether through bathing, setting lights, or self-anointing with oils, this type of work generally involves writing two parallel lists on one sheet of paper. One list is what you don't want, the other is what you wish for. You draw a line between the lists with Lemon juice or Cut and Clear Oil, cut the lists apart, and burn the "bad" list, after which you fold up and keep the "good" list. Bathing with Cut and Clear Bath Crystals in a tub of water with added Black Walnuts greatly enhances this work.

Read more about Cut and Clear work online at:
LuckyMojo.com/cutandclear.html

UNCROSSING HEALTH MATTERS

By far, the most seemingly hopeless cases of crossed conditions that I encounter in my work do not have some extreme versions of magical attack at their root. In nearly every situation where unconquerable spiritual foes seem present is a knot of unresolved emotional and mental energies that a spiritual attack may have exacerbated, but did not cause. This goes similarly for extreme cases of spirit intrusion and demonic possession; the intrusion is often a symptom of internal dis-ease that must be addressed following removal of the offending energy if lasting protection is to be ensured.

Many of us live lives mired in anxiety, self-judgment, shame, and guilt without ever realizing it, being aware only of the patterns that we seem to encounter again and again in our lives. It is incredibly helpful for both workers and laypersons to educate themselves regarding what trauma and emotions are and how they function. Like regular spiritual cleansing and uncrossing, healing might best be seen as an ongoing journey that every individual is on, but it is one that needs our attention. We need not wait for our systems to crash before we take self-mending actions. It requires that we humbly take on life as a teacher and allow ourselves to be present to our pain, how others' words and actions trigger us, and the fact that some days, the cup from which we sip can feel empty. It is from that choice to be present to the hurt and the triggers that we can ask for our cup to be filled.

Most of us do not live in cultures that encourage our wholeness. Neither do we live in cultures with rites of passage that effectively enable us to shed old skins and reveal new glories. Many of our childhood wounds are still with us, and though we might believe that we've "gotten over it," we rarely have. There is a difference between healing and putting up walls, and the way we treat our emotional bodies can not only invite spiritual illness, but keep the intimacy and loving relationships that we seek at bay as well.

Part of self-mastery is being able to admit when we need help. Conjure practitioners often include prayers for health, blessing, and love uncrossing alongside any spells undertaken to adress other conditions, and when in need, they may ask others to set lights for them. It is important to remember that spiritual work for healing is never meant to replace competent medical advice from licensed individuals, but it may be found to be a powerful aid in tandem with mainstream forms of care. It can also help open the doors to finding the most qualified practitioners for the conditions we are facing.

Some common herbs, roots, minerals, and zoological curios called upon for healing and blessing:

- **Althæa Root:** Helps to bring healing, comfort, and spiritual assistance.
- **Angelica Root:** Helps feminine-oriented folks tap into their power.
- **Cowrie Shells:** Has the appearance of a vulva; used for sexual healing and empowerment for feminine-oriented people.
- **Dixie John Root:** Helps cultivate positive relations in the home.
- **Eucalyptus:** Helps bring an end to bad habits and self-jinxing. Wards off enablers and bad influences.
- **Frankincense:** A resin for blessing and invoking divine favour.
- **High John the Conqueror Root:** Strengthens and empowers.
- **Hyssop:** Aids in forgiveness and the assuaging of guilt.
- **Lavender:** Soothingly brings peace, healing, and mental tranquility.
- **Lemon:** Severs emotional ties to persons, places, and events, whether they be past or present experiences.
- **Life Everlasting:** Promotes health and longevity. Can drink as a tea.
- **Marjoram:** Assuages grief and sorrow. Brings happiness to the home.
- **Master Root:** Helpful in cultivating self-control and self-mastery.
- **Rosemary:** Empowers the feminine. Promotes positive family relations.
- **Rose:** Engenders unconditional love for and amongst all beings.
- **Self Heal (All Heal):** Aids in promoting health in all arenas.
- **Solomon Seal Root:** Enhances wisdom, breaks patterns of victimhood.
- **Violet (Heartsease, Pansy):** Helps to soothe the heart.
- **Walnuts:** Effectively sever emotional ties to past persons.

Popular spiritual oils, incenses, baths, and powders used for works of healing and blessing:

- **7-11 Holy Oil:** A Biblical formula for anointing and blessing.
- **Blessing:** For healing and invoking divine grace and favour.
- **Cast Off Evil:** For shedding fear, harmful habits, and bad influences.
- **Crucible of Courage:** For instilling bravery and determination.
- **Cut and Clear:** For shedding emotional attachments.
- **Healing:** For relief of physical, mental, and emotional pain and illness.
- **Peace Water:** For inviting benevolent spirits and instilling peace.
- **Tranquility:** For instilling calmness and gentleness.

CAST OFF EVIL BATH

On a Saturday as the moon wanes, bathe downward in a tea of Lemon, Eucalyptus, and Master Root, or with Cast Off Evil Bath Crystals, affirming that any self-imposed shackles in mind and behavior are removed. Leave the remnant water at a crossroads and dress yourself with King Solomon Wisdom Oil. Do this for nine days.

TO EASE EMOTIONAL PAIN

In times of emotional grief and mourning due to the loss of a loved one or the end of a relationship, place a live Violet plant by your bed. Sit and talk with it, communicating your sorrow and pain. Ask it to help quell your sorrow and thank it for its help. Do this daily while engaging in self-care, such as physical exercise and being around uplifting company. In lieu of a living plant, carry Violet leaves or flowers in a pouch.

SWEETNESS BATH

Sometimes, after cleansing or protection, what one needs is glow. A sweetness bath can uplift your spirits and it can also be a great tool in self-love work, sweetening you to yourself. Take a bowl of honey to a bathtub and rub it all over yourself. When finished, rinse yourself off.

THE WATER OF SEVEN WATERS

As cat yronwode tells it, "The Water of Seven Waters, like Water of Notre Dame and Lourdes Water, is an old formula for bathing rites. It is utilized by women who have cancer, as an adjunct to their regular medical treatments. To make it, water is collected and combined from seven different sources, such as a spring, a river, a well, rainfall, snow, the ocean, and so forth. Catholics living in urban areas may collect Holy Water from seven different churches.

"One need not pilgrimage to collect all of the waters, though; they can be collected by seven people so that each has her own supply. This method is used by women who wish to distribute the water to friends in a similar condition. To share in this rite, collect seven small bottles of water from your sacred source and send six of the bottles by mail to the each of six other women. When they have all seven (including their own) they blend them, and you too will mingle the waters from all six small bottles you receive, plus your own small bottle from your own sacred source, and that gives you a large bottle of all seven waters to bathe in."

TO BRING HEALING TO FAMILY RELATIONS

Make a petition paper by listing the names of all of the family members that are at odds with one another or are living under the same roof and turn that paper ¼ turn clockwise, writing over "Loving Sweetness Together" three times stacked. Anoint the four corners and center of the petition with Healing Oil and place personal concerns such as photos and bits of hair in the center. Add a bit of Dixie John Root, a pinch of Sugar, a pinch of Lavender, and one Balm of Gilead bud for each of the listed family members. Make the paper into a packet by folding it towards you, turning it clockwise, and repeating until it can no longer be folded.

Push your petition paper into a jar of honey and, as you lift your finger out of the jar, put it to your lips and lick, saying "As this honey tastes sweet to me, so are we sweetened to one another by God's grace." If there have been quarrels between family members, shake up a bottle of Peace Water and add a drop or two on of the top the honey. Place the lid back on the jar and, every Friday, dress a white crucifix candle with Healing Oil and burn it on top while praying Psalms 96.

SKULL CANDLE FOR MENTAL HEALING

(from Hoodoo Bible Magic by Miss Michaele and Professor Porterfield)

Take a small square of white paper and write out on it Deuteronomy 31:8: *"And the Lord, he it is that doth go before thee; he will be with thee, he will not fail thee, neither forsake thee: fear not, neither be dismayed."*

Turn the paper clockwise and write your name seven times over the Bible verse. Dress the paper by making a five spot pattern of small crosses on it with Cast Off Evil Oil. Then place a few White or Yellow Mustard Seeds, a pinch of Five Finger Grass, and a crumb of Dragon's Blood resin in the paper. Fold it toward you, then turn it and fold it again. With a knife or other sharp object, carve a hole in the bottom of a white skull candle large enough to hold the folded paper packet. Melt the left-over wax in a spoon and use it to seal the hole back up. Burn the candle in sections for at least a half an hour a day while reciting Deuteronomy 31:9 and Psalms 23. A skull candle burned this way will last for weeks.

A MOJO HAND FOR HEALTH

Combine Self-Heal, Angelica Root, and Life Everlasting in a white flannel bag. Feed with whiskey once a week to stay in good health.

A SPIRITUAL CHURCH RITE FOR HEALING NATURE

This spell was shared by Rev. catherine yronwode of Missionary Independent Spiritual Church for the healing of the Gulf of Mexico after the BP Oil Spill of 2010. It can be adapted for use with any other similar environmental disaster caused by petroleum spills.

"Create an altar for the place, the people, the animals, the plants. Gather pictures, mementos, whatever helps you focus.

"Now, here is where it goes counter to what you probably thought i would suggest. DO NOT USE CANDLES ON THIS ALTAR unless they are made from 100% beeswax. Do not use petroleum based candles on this altar! In fact, i would not use any candles at all.

"Place clear glass bowls or glasses of water on the altar — i was told by Spirit to use seven of them. Glass custard cups or wine glasses will do, as long as they are clean glass with no writing or pictures on them (cut glass is okay). If possible fill them with water from seven sources (spring, river, ocean, rain, well, lake, holy water), but if that is too daunting, use clean spring water and ocean water mixed together.

"Set these seven bowls or glasses out in a rainbow arc on the altar. Into each bowl put a small crucifix, while speaking aloud a prayer for relief. The crucifixes may be small or large, as long as getting wet will not hurt them. Pray continually as you do this, and i recommend the 23rd Psalm, and a call for help to Jesus Christ.

"Pray at this altar for three days for your specific needs in regard to the Gulf waters, the animals, the plants, and the people of the region. On the third day, take the seven bowls or glasses to the ocean and, one by one, empty them in, keeping the crucifixes, symbolically cleansing the ocean, in the name of Jesus Christ, a fisherman, amen.

"If you do not live near the Gulf, you may pour the bowls or glasses of water into any live stream of running water, but as you empty each one, first speak aloud your understanding that all waters run to the sea, and all the seas are one, then remove the crucifix, and say your prayer for cleansing the ocean, in the name of Jesus Christ, a fisherman, amen.

"The seven crucifixes may be gifted to seven friends with instructions for this rite, in the expectation that each of them will acquire six more crucifixes and do the same, and thus spread the rite around the world, or, if you prefer, the crucifixes may be given to those in need of spiritual help in this time of crisis."

UNCROSSING LEGAL MATTERS

"The master's tools will never dismantle the master's house."
— Audre Lorde, feminist and civil rights activist

The racial and economic injustice faced by the Black community since the arrival of enslaved Africans to the United States has always been a microcosm of the broader injustices that are used to maintain hierarchies of power in capitalist and other societies. Out of the need for self-preservation, folk magic tools and techniques have been wielded by the common people to thwart despotic and unjust power in cultures all around the world, and these old-time tricks can be just as helpful today as they were in times past.

Spiritual work for legal matters begins with protection, such as Law Keep Away tricks to remain invisible to legal and other authorities. The next line of defense consists of Stop Gossip spells to protect from both false and revealing testimony, and Confusion spells to sow dissent and delay court proceedings. Court Case spells work by directly affecting the thoughts of judges, lawyers, jury members, probation officers, and opposing parties through works of influence. Custody cases may involve King Solomon Wisdom spells, as Solomon was a wise Biblical judge who ruled fairly in a similar matter. Pay Me spells are performed to enhance the sympathy given to a plaintiff, while for a defendant, there is also the important matter of divine favour, such as Just Judge spiritual workings that appeal to that Highest Judge in the Court of the Heaven for the delivery of a fair sentence, or merely for grace.

Not every root doctor is gifted at shifting the odds of legal proceedings, and such situations can seem overwhelming to the magical novice. When planning legal magic strategy, it is helpful to remember and to be aware of the key human targets involved in the case — not only the judge, jury, and lawyers, but also witnesses, court reporters, bailiffs, and jailers. The paper trail of official documents and the public availability of photographs on the internet make for excellent personal concerns and spell materials.

Read more about court case spells and what you can do if you have been arrested at this web page:
LuckyMojo.com/courtcase.html
Additional spells for legal matters can be found at the Lucky Mojo Esoteric Archive online at:
LuckyMojo.com/spells/purple/courtcasespells.html

Some common herbs, roots, minerals, and zoological curios called upon for legal and court case matters:

- **Alum Powder:** For shutting the mouths of opponents in court.
- **Black Mustard Seed:** For confusion and disruption in legal proceedings.
- **Calendula:** For luck in court proceedings that involve financial issues.
- **Cascara Sagrada:** Brings luck and divine favour in legal matters.
- **Calamus Root:** For asserting control over persons and situations.
- **Celandine:** Keeps off the law and confuses testimony by law officers.
- **Deer's Tongue:** For enhancing the eloquence of your lawyer or yourself.
- **Indian Head Cents:** Used as "scouts" that keep away the law.
- **Licorice Root:** For asserting control over persons and situations.
- **Little John to Chew (Galangal):** The premiere botanical in legal work, often chewed on-site and in real-time during court proceedings.
- **Oregano:** Keeps away the law and wards of meddling individuals.
- **Poppy Seeds:** A popular curio for causing confusion.
- **Sugar:** To sweeten a judge, probation or parole officer, or case worker.
- **Sumac:** For instilling harmony, to have a judge and jury look favourably upon you, for receiving mercy of the court if you are guilty.
- **Tobacco:** To influence, appease, and control people and situations.

Popular spiritual oils, incenses, baths, and powders used for works involving the law and court case issues:

- **Essence of Bend Over:** For bending others to your will.
- **Blessing:** For invoking divine favour.
- **Commanding:** For bringing others under your command.
- **Confusion:** For inflicting mental calamity upon others.
- **Court Case**: For victory in all types of legal proceedings.
- **Hot Foot:** For removal of a party, such as a judge, lawyer, or witness.
- **Inflammatory Confusion:** To turn confusion into anger and discord.
- **Influence:** For affecting the thoughts and emotions of others.
- **Just Judge:** For fair and compassionate sentencing.
- **King Solomon Wisdom:** For wise and just custody decisions.
- **Law Keep Away:** For protection and invisibility from legal figures.
- **Pay Me:** To receive a settlement on a claim of money owed.
- **Stop Gossip:** To end slander and shut the mouths of opponents.

TO STOP A FORECLOSURE OR EVICTION

To keep oneself from being evicted from a space, get a Railroad Spike for each corner of the property and anoint them with Protection Oil. Drive it into the ground at each spot, saying "I will NEVER be forced to leave this home," effectively "nailing down your house." Some folks take this a step further by sprinkling a bit of their urine on the spot as an assertion of their claim on the territory and by placing an Indian Head Cent face-up atop the head of each of spike to function as lookouts regarding authorities who may try to thwart you by sneaky means. Folks who have access to the graves of Ancestors with whom they had good relationships while they were alive (or whom they know were loving and protective) may purchase a handful of dirt from their graves with a silver dime and a glug of whiskey. These folks will sprinkle a bit of this dirt over each Railroad Spike while calling on this Ancestor to ensure that their home is kept from being taken. Dirt from the grave of a beloved pet, especially guard animals, can also come in handy.

If you live in an apartment or other dwelling without outdoor access, this working can be effectively performed by anointing household nails with Protection Oil and nailing them into the floor in each corner on the inside of the premises. This working can also be performed for businesses. Be sure to follow it up with works employing products such as Blessing (for divine favour on your behalf), Block Buster (to crush obstacles standing in your path), or Fast Luck (to quickly attract that which is needed). Ensure that you and your space remain in a spiritually cleansed and protected state.

LEMON COURT CASE WORKING

For a good outcome to a court case, cut a Lemon in half, sprinkling salt on one half and wrapping it in a new linen cloth. Repeat with the other half and put one in your pocket or handbag. Before entering the courtroom, rub one of these on your hands towards yourself. When entering the courtroom, take the other half and squirt it onto your hand while reciting Psalms 23.

LITTLE JOHN TO CHEW, THE COURT CASE ROOT

Little John to Chew, popularly known as Galangal, is the premiere botanical called upon in legal matters in the hoodoo tradition, so much so that it is often simply called Court Case Root. Boil with a bit of sugar to soften it and chew it on the day of proceedings, rubbing spit onto the furniture of the courtroom while praying for your case or the case of a loved one.

BEEF TONGUE SPELL TO SHUT UP OPPONENTS IN COURT

This working can be used to stop gossip in any environment, but is particularly popular in legal matters for shutting the mouths of those whose words could damage your case. To perform it, get a whole cow tongue from a butcher and cut a slit down the center. Insert the names and personal concerns of anyone whose testimony or opinion could work against you. It is not easy to acquire truly personal concerns of everyone you know is involved, but in court cases, names written with strong intention often suffice quite aptly. Cross the names with the words "SHUT THE FUCK UP." Sew the slit with black thread and sprinkle the tongue with Stop Gossip Powders and Alum Powder. Take a string and anoint it with Stop Gossip Oil before wrapping up the tongue while saying "You shut your mouths. You are bound from speaking against me." Burn a dressed black candle directly on the tongue. If you'd like, you can surround it with brown glass-encased vigil candles dressed with Court Case Oil. When finished, place the tongue in a freezer or dispose of it in a cemetery.

TO CONFUSE AN OPPOSING ATTORNEY

This spell is used to directly thwart the efforts of an opposing attorney, or other legal authority whom it serves to confuse rather than sweeten. Confused opponents suffer from lost paperwork, verbal fumbling, and embarrassing mistakes that weaken their credibility and impair their ability.

On the back of the person's business card or photo, write his or her name nine times, stacked. Turn the paper turn counterclockwise, and write the word "CONFUSION" once over names. (Alternatively, write the names every-which-way and write "CONFUSION" twice across them in the form of an X.)

Anoint this petition with Confusion or Inflammatory Confusion Oil in a five-spot pattern and place Poppy Seed, Black Mustard Seed, and Red Pepper in the center. Fold the paper away from yourself, turn it counterclockwise, and fold it again to make a packet. Remove some of the wax from the bottom of a black skull candle and load it with the petition, melting the wax back over it. Like a doll-baby, baptise the loaded candle in the name of the target and breathe it to life. Wash the candle in vinegar and burn it a little while over a period of nine days while cursing the target's mental ability, specifically in regards your case. You can dip pins and needles in Confusion Oil and insert them into the candle's top, eyes, and ears to negate the use of their senses. Be sure to use a cleansing regimen after each session.

DEALING WITH INTRUSIVE SPIRITS AND ENERGIES

Not everyone can do this sort of work for themselves, but here are some spells to try. If negative spirits cannot be dislodged, or if they return despite your work, you may need to seek the help of a professional root doctor, spiritworker, exorcist priest, or shamanic healer, according to the ways of your religion, personal beliefs, or cultural training.

DR. E.'S SPIRIT TRAP TO CAPTURE SPIRITS OF THE DEAD
This spell was taught to me by my mentor and friend, the late Dr. E.

To remove a spirit of the dead from a person, take a dark-coloured bottle and add ½-inch of beer to it, or pour out the contents of a beer bottle until that much is left. Add a pinch of Mugwort, asking it to be potent, and gently swirl the mixture around to create an intoxicating spirit treat. Then add nine pins or nails and pieces of thorny or stinging plants such as Cactus, Barberry, Nettles, Holly, or Blackberry. You don't need all of these plants, but as you add each one, ask it to catch and keep anything that enters inside the bottle.

Place the bottle on a dark cloth in front of the person experiencing the spirit intrusion. Have a cork, the original bottle cap, or a little bundle of Espanta Muerto herb ready. Light a cigar and tell the spirit that you are sure it must be tired and in need of sustenance, and that such sustenance has been made available in the bottle directly before it. While saying this, blow smoke on the person in a downward fashion toward the top of the bottle. You are luring the spirit into the trap. At some point, you may hear a "whoosh" or "pop" sound of the spirit entering the bottle. I usually see the shape of the smoke above the bottle change into a funnel, at which point I know that the spirit has entered.

Quickly use a yes-no form of divination, such as a coin or shell toss, a one-card cut, or a pendulum, to ensure that the spirit has been lured into the bottle then cork or cap it. Wrap the cloth around the bottle and use a cord to further bind the bundle. Bring it to a cemetery and leave nine coins at the gate before entering. Once inside, dig a hole and bury the bottle with prayers for the spirit. You may make a second coin offering to the guardians of the gate upon exiting, to ensure the spirit is kept.

Immediate attention to blessing and protection on behalf of the client should follow this, and the client should be sent home with tools for further work, such as a series of Uncrossing or Jinx Killer baths, or condition oils like Blessing, Protection, or Road Opener that pertain to his or her needs.

TRICKSTER SPIRIT DISCOURAGING INCENSE

In "Communing with the Spirits" by Martin Coleman we are told that to send away trickster spirits, you can combine two parts Frankincense — a holy resin that uplifts the energetic vibration of any space — with one part Tobacco, preferably from a crushed cigar, and burn it on a lit charcoal disk.

INTRUSIVE SPIRIT REMOVAL BATH

Combine Salt, Rue, and a pinch of Tobacco and use this mix for at least seven days as an uncrossing bath-tea while calling upon your Helping Spirits to aid in the removal of any and all intrusive spirit energies. Dress yourself with a blend of Protection and Blessing Oil following each bath.

TO STOP HAG RIDING

From Mrs. S. in South Carolina, via "Voodoo and Hoodoo" by Jim Haskins, we learn how to stop hag-riding. Place equal amounts of Mustard Seed and Flax Seed in a sifter and set it on one side of your bed. On the other side, set a pan of cold water. Since hags like neither cold water nor Mustard and Flax Seeds, they will trouble you no more. This speaks to the widespread belief that spiritual intruders are forced to count nearby objects, including holes in a sifter, slowing them down and inevitably confusing them.

FOUR WAYS TO PROTECT A SPACE WHILE YOU SLEEP

Placing Cedarwood or Camphor in the corners of a room discourages low-vibration entities from entering. In lieu of these Vick's VapoRub, known for its camphorous scent, may be used to dress both the corners and the bedposts.

A Bible open to Psalms 121 placed under the bed keeps off night-spirits.

Vinegar is displeasing to spirits of the dead. Pour some into cups and leave a cup in each corner of the space until the entity is gone.

Protection Oil dabbed at the four corners of every bedroom window and door wards off attempts by enemies to send disturbing dreams your way.

BOTTLE TREES AS SPIRIT TRAPS

The construction of blue glass bottle trees is a traditional way to protect from intrusive spirits. Construction consists either of jamming bottles directly onto the branches of a tree, or hanging them with wire or string. If one falls, this is regarded as a sign that a spirit has been caught and dealt with, though it might be wise to consider additional precautionary measures.

REVERSING AND PROTECTION

All too often, preventative measures are overlooked until harm has already occurred and it's too late. This pattern is as common in the realm of folk magic as it is in the mundane world, though on the bright side, if we are observant, these experiences often show us where we are most vulnerable and in need of additional defenses.

Reversing work sends back to its senders any harm that was inflicted on the spiritual or mundane planes. To do this, petitions for Divine Justice may be used along with the praying of Psalms. Reversing spells may involve writing backward or using physical mirrors to reflect and return spiritual energies. If the perpetrators are shrouded in mystery, the phrase "All enemies both known and unknown" is employed.

Protection prayers, talismans, and spells are a necessity for any practitioner of the spiritual arts and should be a staple for every individual and every home. They may be pre-emptive and apotropaic, or they may be employed to ensure continued blessings after an uncrossing rite has been completed. In hoodoo we find workings for warding spaces against human and spiritual intruders and guarding folks against physical injury, illness, curses, hexes, jinxes, gossip, and the evil eye. Regular household products as well as specialized spiritual supplies form an arsenal with which to protect ourselves, our homes, and our families, both in familiar territory and on the road.

Divination can be helpful in ascertaining the source of the attack and may reveal which means of remediation would be most effective toward limiting the damage done and recovering a quickly as possible. A reader may also be able to determine who, out of several possibilities, actually cast the curse and whether the work can be reversed back to the sender or if the sender is shielded from retaliatory attacks.

A person's initial experience of being spiritually attacked can be confusing and worrisome as watching one's life respond to the intentional malice of others can trigger a sense of loss of control, inducing panic. I have often told my clients that the first and best response to confirmation of spiritual attack is to laugh. Laughter asserts sovereignty in the face of adversity, affirms power and victory, and disperses energy. Aside from this, it wise to take immediate action based on divinatory guidance and to avoid consulting divination in extreme amounts. Remaining calm and disciplined in thought and in action is your primary shield while in a state of recovery.

Some common herbs, roots, minerals, and zoological curios called upon reversing and protection:

- **Agrimony:** Said to reverse curses and jinxes that have been cast.
- **Alum Powder:** As it puckers the tongue, so it closes wicked mouths.
- **Angelica Root:** Like an angel, it guards persons, spaces, and children.
- **Aspand:** Burned on charcoal, it protects against the evil eye.
- **Basil:** It is said that where Basil is, evil cannot be.
- **Bay Laurel:** Wards against evil and is placed around spells and in the corners of rooms to keep one's spiritual work from being detected.
- **Black Pepper:** Wards off evil witchcraft and jinxes.
- **Comfrey Root:** A protector of travelers from harmful strangers.
- **Crab Shell Powder:** Used in works of reversing harmful energies, mimicking how crabs are seen to walk in a sideways manner.
- **Devil's Shoe Strings:** It trips up the Devil and any evil coming your way.
- **Garlic:** Discourages troublesome visitors and keeps the law away.
- **Grains of Paradise:** Sewn into small packets to protect the home.
- **High John the Conqueror Root:** Protects by strengthening you.
- **Mercury Dime:** An apotropaic charm that warns of danger.
- **Oregano:** Said to protect by keeping away meddling individuals.
- **Rue:** Protects from witchcraft and the evil eye.

Popular spiritual oils, incenses, baths, and powders used in works of reversing and protection:

- **Banishing:** Sends bad people and spirits away and keeps them there.
- **Devil's Shoe String:** Ties down the Devil and also human enemies.
- **Fear Not to Walk Over Evil:** Protects from tricks laid on the ground.
- **Fiery Wall of Protection:** Singes intruding foes and enemies.
- **Four Thieves Vinegar:** An edible concoction popular for warding off disease, it also protects from spiritual harm and unnatural illness.
- **Hot Foot:** For banishing from a premises, job, or social situation.
- **Protection:** A calm, cool formula for warding and guarding.
- **Reversing:** Sends harm that has been done right back to its sender.
- **Run Devil Run:** Said to drive the Devil (and the devilish) away.
- **Safe Travel:** For safety on a journey and for a happy welcome home.
- **Stop Gossip:** To end slander and shut the mouths of opponents.

REVERSING EVIL WITH WATER AND THE PSALMS

You will need privacy to do this spell. Fill a glass halfway up with water. If you have Reversing Oil, add a drop to the water, but it's okay if you do not. Take a plate and the glass of water to your front door (from inside your home) and place the plate on top of the glass. Holding this in your hands, pray aloud with strong conviction that any and all harm sent to you, your home, or your family is now "reversed" unto its senders. On the word "reversed," turn the glass of water and plate upside down so that the water is trapped between the plate and the glass. It is okay if a little bit seeps out.

Place the trapped water on the floor near the front door. Open your Bible to Psalms 91. Read this aloud while holding a butcher knife in your hand, pointed toward the door. If you have Reversing or Protection Oil, you may anoint the knife. Turn to Psalms 101 and read this aloud as well. (It may help to read these Psalms to yourself beforehand in order to understand what it is about these scriptures that will help defend you and turn negative energy away from yourself, your home, and your loved ones. Use this understanding in order to punctuate where it feels appropriate while praying aloud.)

When finished, lay your knife across Psalms 101 with the point facing your door. Place this near the overturned glass — and make sure it remains child- and pet-proof. If this is impossible, the work can be performed at a distance, in a private room, but all gestures and prayers should be made toward the entrance door, with the knife pointed in this direction as well.

If you are under serious attack, perform the work for nine days. You may also light candles dressed with Reversing Oil directly on top of the overturned glass. These could be tealights or butted and reversed double-action candles. As they burn, affirm and believe that all harm sent toward you, your home, and your family is fully reversed toward its senders.

Once you and your loved ones are no longer in harm's way, carry the glass and plate to a crossroads and remove the plate from under the glass, spilling the water out and asking the spirit of the crossroads to aid in reversing the harm sent toward yourself and your family. Go home without looking back and thoroughly clean the plate, glass, and knife.

REVERSING EVIL WITH A CONVEX LENS CAR MIRROR

If your neighbours are evil, get a 3-inch convex lens "blind spot" car mirror, dress the surface with an X of Reversing Oil, and glue it to the outside of your house, facing in their direction. Renew the X at every full moon.

REVERSING EVIL WITH A MIRROR BOX SPELL

To stop someone who is harming you, your home, or a loved one via spiritual or mundane means, place a photo of the person between two mirrors in which you've never seen your reflection, mirror sides inward. Do this by the light of a single black or double action candle that you have butted. Tie or tape the two mirrors together while telling the person that any and all harm they have or could cause is reversed back to them and that they are caught in a trap of their own making. Place the candle in a holder on top of the mirror-packet and, after it finishes burning, take the packet to a cemetery. Pay nine coins at the entrance before entering and bury the packet at the grave of a spirit who you pay to ensure that this is carried out. A yes / no form of divination with your Helping Spirits can assist you to find a spirit who is willing and able to carry out the job. A silver dime and a shot of whiskey is a fine payment. Perform an uncrossing bath when you get home.

A more severe form of this spell is to make a small black cloth doll-baby of your enemy and load it with the foe's personal concerns and a petition that the enemy be bound and have all harm sent back. Blindfold the doll before bringing it to life through baptism and breath and bind it up with string or chain while stating that you bind the person in every way and on every plane of existence from ever causing harm again. It is helpful to be specific here: bind the hands while stating that the foe cannot use them to harm you, and bind the feet while stating that the enemy cannot run to others for aid to harm you or undo this work. Next, take a small cardboard or wood box and glue shards of a mirror in which you have never looked at your own reflection on the inside, along the bottom, sides, and top. Cracks between the shards are okay. Sprinkle powders such as Reversing and Hot Foot, or curios such as Crab Shell Powder, Agrimony, Red Pepper, Black Pepper, and Oregano on the doll. Some folks add more volatile elements depending on the severity of the situation. Close the box and wrap it up tightly with cord. Burn candles on or around this box while affirming that this person's harm has completely been sent back to them and that they are incapable of harming you or your loved ones again. Bury it in the cemetery and take an uncrossing bath.

TO BAR ENEMIES FROM YOUR THRESHOLD

To bar enemies from entering a space, sprinkle a line of finely ground Red Brick Dust at the threshold. It is said that foes cannot cross it. Alternately, nail a line of nine Devil's Shoe Strings into the floor across the entrance.

TO PROTECT A HOME'S INHABITANTS

Take the 10 of Clubs out of the deck of cards and write a list of all of the home's inhabitants in the center. Touch each club on the card while saying the name of one of Jesus's 12 Apostles along with the phrase "Protect and fortify us." Wrap the card around a whole Angelica Root with white string and keep in a white flannel bag on the inside of the home near the front door. Feed the bag once per week with whiskey or Fiery Wall of Protection Oil.

PROTECTION MOJO

Combine Bay Leaf, Devil's Shoe Strings, and Rue in a red flannel bag. Breathe it to life, name it, and feed it whiskey, Protection, or Fiery Wall of Protection Oil once a week. Keep it pinned inside your clothing against your skin for a week aside from showering and sleeping during which you can keep it pinned to the inside of your pillow. Afterwards, keep in a safe place.

PROTECTION, BLESSING, AND ALL-PURPOSE OIL

Take a small amount of Olive Oil and pray Psalms 23 over it, ensuring that your breath touches the oil itself. Keep in a cool, dry place, and if you want it ensure its longevity, add a squirt of Vitamin E or Jojoba oil to it. This is a fantastic oil for protection, blessing, money, and all good works.

TO STOP EVIL FROM ENTERING YOUR HOME

(from Hoodoo Herb and Root Magic by catherine yronwode)

Mix Sandalwood powder with Angelica Root powder and sprinkle the mix across the front of your house or place a whole Angelica Root and Sandalwood chips in a muslin bag inside the house near the front door to repel both evil people and evil spirits.

TO PROTECT A SPACE FROM THE EVIL EYE

To ward off the effects that covetous people could have on your life from entering your home or business, hang a nazar evil eye charm outside the door or inside the space directly facing the front door. To empower it, wash it in an infusion of Rue or smoke it in either Rue or Aspand before hanging it.

HOUSE PROTECTION WITH RUE

Hang dried Rue stalks or a flannel bag filled with Rue above the door frame inside your home to ward off evil and spiritual attacks.

BOTANICALS FOR PROTECTING TO THE HOME

Basil and Black Snake Root can be sprinkled around the home and prayerfully swept out the door to protect a home against intruders and evil.

A small cloth packet filled with Grains of Paradise, to which an image of Archangel Micahel is glued, may be placed at each door for protection.

Whole Angelica Root, Bay Leaf, and Salt have popularly been placed in the corners of a room or a home to ward against harm. If a center rug is present, The same materials can be placed under it as well to invoke the five-spot, or the transformative power of the crossroads.

LEMON FREEZER SPELL FOR PROTECTION

To stop a person from harassing you or to get them off your back (not move them to another location, per se), take a sheet of aluminum foil and place a Lemon on top. Make a slit in the Lemon and insert a petition with a statement such as "LEAVE ME ALONE" or "BACK OFF" written across their name along with their photo or personal concerns. You can also copy out Psalms 37 if you like to work with scriptural passages. Add a pinch of Black Pepper, Red Pepper, and Oregano. Pin the slit together with nine pins or needles. Sprinkle a bit of your urine on this to dominate the person and wrap the Lemon in the foil by rolling it away from you. Throw the mess in the back of your freezer, slamming the door shut. If the person is a gossiper, add some Alum Powder in the spell to shut them up.

FOR PROTECTION WHILE YOU SLEEP

To protect against spirit intrusions and spiritual attacks during the night, keep a Bible open to Psalms 91 under your bed with a pair of open metal scissors laid over the pages. You may anoint the scissors with a protection oil. A Bible once owned by a beloved family member is said to hold power and would be appropriate in such a working. To keep it clean, cover it with clear plastic or, more traditionally, a white cloth.

A PERSONAL PROTECTION WASH

(from "Hoodoo Herb and Root Magic" by catherine yronwode)

Boil Basil in water, strain out the leaves, and wipe yourself downward with a white handkerchief dipped in the water. Do this every morning for nine days. On the last day, throw the remaining bath water out your front door, and your enemies cannot harm you.

Carrying the Good Work On

Those who do not have power over the story that dominates their lives, the power to retell it, rethink it, deconstruct it, joke about it, and change it as times change, truly are powerless, because they cannot think new thoughts.
— Salman Rushdie

When calamity strikes by way of happenstance or overt attack, we are hit the hardest where we are most vulnerable, but once we are delivered and we have broken the jinx, taken off crossed conditions, lifted the curse, or walked away from a mess, our next immediate need is to understand what happened and engage the aid of allies to help us from suffering such setbacks again.

UNLOCKING CLARITY AND SELF-MASTERY

In hoodoo, we find tools and techniques not only for cultivating power and developing personal mastery, but for attuning ourselves to the wisdom of our guides and our Helping Spirits, without whom we may find ourselves out to sea without a compass. They remember our soul's purpose — who we came here to be in spite of the break ups, setbacks, and lost soul parts — and they can help us put ourselves back together as well as provide daily guidance, protection, and comfort in the storms that life, the great teacher, brings our way. They remember the path we chose — the way toward the fulfillment of our heart's deepest desires — and can bring us the messages we need to help us get back on track no matter how far we believe we've veered from who we came here to be.

With their aid and that of allies in the ancestral, plant, mineral, and animal kingdoms, we can stay the course and find that a conspiracy truly does exist to bless our very socks off.

In order to find our allies, we need clarity of vision. Clarity allows us to see the road that lies ahead, to perceive friends, family, and loved ones for who they truly are, and to recognize our blessings when they arrive.

In order to walk beside our spirit allies, we need the power of self-mastery and self-control. We must shed self-talk of victimhood and take our places among those whose will is strong and whose progress is toward a goal, not toward self-pity and decay.

Some common herbs, roots, minerals, animalia, and other curios called upon for cultivating clarity, mastery, and power:

- **Althæa Root:** Invokes benevolent spiritual guidance and aid.
- **Acacia:** Burned to invoke visions and communicate with the deceased.
- **Anise Seed:** Enhances seership and psychic abilities.
- **Angelica Root:** Connects to angels and women Ancestors.
- **Bay Leaf:** Aids dreams, visions, and increases chances of victory.
- **Bergamot Orange:** Increases personal power in spite of authority.
- **Eyebright:** Brings clarity. Anoint eyelids and head with tea infusion.
- **Flax Seed:** Enhances mental power and induces visions and dreams.
- **High John the Conqueror Root:** Masculine strength and inner will.
- **Master Root:** Grants mastery by bringing oneself into self-alignment.
- **Master of the Woods:** Helps cultivate motivation and royal authority.
- **Mugwort:** Aids in psychic work and prophetic dreaming.
- **Queen Elizabeth Root:** Feminine power and sovereignty.
- **Rosemary:** Promotes clarity. Empowers feminine-oriented folks.
- **Sage:** An herb of wisdom, sagacity, and feminine power.
- **Sampson Snake Root:** Empowers and enhances masculine nature.
- **Solomon Seal Root:** Aids mental faculties and wise decision-making.
- **Star Anise:** Aids psychic visioning and helps one to dream true.
- **Tobacco:** Helps one make contact with spiritual entities.

Popular spiritual oils, incenses, baths, and powders used for works of clarity and self- mastery:

- **9-Herb Bath:** For wisdom, strength, and mastery.
- **Clarity:** For thwarting confusion and gaining deep insight into matters.
- **Crucible of Courage:** For instilling bravery and determination.
- **Indian Spirit Guide:** To foster connections to Native Ancestors.
- **John the Conqueror:** For empowering in spite of the odds.
- **King Solomon Wisdom:** For being as wise as the Biblical figure.
- **Master:** For developing temporal and social power.
- **Master Key:** For developing spiritual and occult power.
- **Power:** For increasing personal will and spiritual potency.
- **Psychic Vision:** For increasing intuitive abilities and spiritual insight.
- **Spirit Guide:** For calling forth benevolent, helpful spirits.

TECHNIQUES FOR INVITING CLARITY
Add a few drops of Rosemary essential oil to a bottle of shampoo or conditioner with the intention that your mind remains clear and strong. To understand a situation more clearly, a cool tea of Eyebright can be brushed in the eyelids for three days, with prayers for signs and guidance.

FOR CLARITY ABOUT ONE'S SPIRITUAL PATH
(from Spiritual Cleansing by Draja Mickarahic)
Make one cup of a Rue infusion and add to a half-filled bathtub. Soak in the tub for eight minutes and perform five full immersions. Pray for spiritual cleansing as well as clarity about one's spiritual path.

FOR GUIDANCE ON LIFE'S JOURNEY
On a piece of paper, write out Psalms 119:105, which reads *"Thy word is a lamp unto my feet, and a light unto my path."* Burn this paper to ashes and mix the ashes with Clarity and Spirit Guide Sachet Powder. Sprinkle in your shoes or the shoes of a loved one whose course needs guidance.

MASTERY CANDLE WORKING
Make a petition paper by writing your name nine times across the word "Self-Mastery" written nine times. Anoint the corners and center with Master Oil (for temporal power) or Master Key Oil (for spiritual power), plus John the Conqueror Oil and King Solomon Wisdom Oil. Add one of your hairs, preferably from your head. Fold the paper towards yourself to make a packet. Put it aside. Carve your name up the spine of a white figural candle to represent yourself and carve the word "Mastery" across the forehead, the chest, and the base. Dress the candle with each oil, stroking toward yourself. Place it on a heatproof dish with three dressed purple candles in a triangle around it. Outline the triangle with Master of the Woods herb and place the packet within it. Burn the candles a few minutes daily over nine Thursdays. Carry the packet in a mojo hand, such as the "Master Mojo," below.

"MASTER MOJO"
(from Hoodoo Herb and Root Magic by catherine yronwode)
To gain personal strength and will power, and also to perform well in sports, carry a red "Master Mojo" that contains Master Root, Master of the Woods, and Sampson Snake Root. Dress it with John the Conqueror Oil.

WHEN YOU ARE STUCK: BLOCK BUSTER WORK

Different practitioners have different ways of viewing block buster work. Some see it as synonymous with road opener or uncrossing work while others view it as especially useful when resolving unrequited love. I consider myself to have a special relationship with block buster work informed by an experience of crossed conditions that I was under many years ago. My take on its applications, therefore, comes from my own experience, though I'm sure it makes a helpful remedy in a wide variety of situations.

Whereas Road Opener Oil carries the energy of clearing the way, like shears to an overgrown hedge, Block Buster Oil is the energy of dynamite applied to a dam. I've found block busting useful when conditions are severe enough to thwart the efficacy of simple acts of uncrossing and when a solution to a problem is muddied by confusion, especially when the nature of the problem itself is difficult to detect. It is additionally helpful in matters where a catch-22 seems to be at play, for instance, needing resources in order to relocate, but needing to relocate in order to acquire resources.

The 8 of Swords card in the Rider-Waite-Smith tarot is a divinatory sign that I associate with the need for block buster work. It depicts a woman bound up and surrounded by menacing blades. A common story told by cartomancers is that the woman is quite easily able to escape from her situation, given the looseness of her bindings. This tells us to remember that it is not only external conditions that can hold us back from what we want and need, for in spite of all the trappings befitting a hostage situation, what the bound young woman in the 8 of Swords card lacks, and is sorely in need of, is courage. But although the likelihood of self-sabotage cannot be overstated, it is certainly not the lone possible obstacle ever standing in our path — after all, someone bound her up and placed those swords around her.

WORKING WITH BLOCK BUSTER SPIRITUAL SUPPLIES

Block Buster Oil and Sachet Powders can be used to dress glass-encased Block Buster vigil lights or plain candles of any size before setting them on a petition paper. Bathing rites performed with Block Buster Bath Crystals may be beneficial as well. Block Buster can be mixed with Road Opener, and I find that Block Buster also pairs well with Clarity and Blessing products, and with Crucible of Courage as well. Regular prayer and petitioning of the Holy Powers for their intercession is strongly suggested in all Block Buster work.

HAWTHORN BERRIES AS A BLOCK BUSTER

One approach to Block Buster work when self-sabotage is at play (most assuredly unbeknownst to the person in need of it) is the long-term administering of Hawthorn leaves and berries in the form of a daily tea, tincture dosage, or carried in a pouch as an herbal ally, though thorough research should always be conducted before imbibing herbal medicines. Hawthorn strengthens the heart both medicinally and spiritually, emboldening us against fear and enabling action where stagnation may have once appeared as the only option available.

NINE-DAY BLOCK BUSTER SPELL

For this spell, you'll need a brick, a marker pen, a hammer, and black cloth. Identify your actual need and write on the brick all of the things you "know" or imagine to be standing in your way. For instance, you could write "I don't have enough money," "I'm cursed," "I'm jinxed," "I'm too tired to try," "This is impossible," "I don't have a driver's license," "I'm too old," "I'm too young," "I didn't finish high school," "My life is a mess," and anything else that might come to mind regarding what is standing between you and your needs or goals. Cover every inch of the brick to the best of your ability and feel free to repeat yourself.

Next, wrap the brick in the black cloth so that there are a few layers around it and take it outdoors to a place where you won't be disturbed. Allow yourself to fully feel the frustration, pain, anger, and sadness you're experiencing about the situation and pour that into the bundle until your words and feelings run dry. Then, take your hammer and use it break the bundled-up brick — but not entirely.

Continue the outpouring of emotion followed by the breaking apart of the brick for the next eight days. On the ninth day, take what remains of the bundle and dispose of it in a running body of water, asking the river or stream to carry away every obstacle standing in the way of your needs.

AMMONIA BLOCK BUSTER SPELL

Take a small bottle and strip of paper the width of the inside circumference of the bottle. On a single line spanning the width of the paper, write the words "Crossed Conditions." Place this piece of paper inside the jar with words facing inwards. Fill the jar with ammonia, cap it tightly, and turn it upside down. Leave it until conditions have brightened.

WHEN YOU ARE READY: ROAD OPENER WORK

Road opening is performed to attract opportunity and invite energy to flow into stagnant areas in life. It is not a form of uncrossing, but it can be a helpful aid if, after crossed conditions have been successfully removed, the areas of luck, money, or love have remained stagnant.

Used alone or added to any money, success, attraction, or love-drawing products, Road Opener supplies can be employed to grant the way into social niches, new financial markets in business, or aid those who are passionate about travel by inviting opportunities and contacts in far-off places. Artists and writers who seek to get noticed by agents and publishers can use Road Opener or call upon the plant Abre Camino; to make sure their work gets seen, Look Me Over products can be blended in as well, to provide a boost.

HOW TO GATHER DIRT FROM A CROSSROADS

Spell casting with oils, powders, incenses, baths, and candles is a powerful way to open your roads, but so is work performed directly at a crossroads — a place where two roads intersect perpendicular to one another.

Many workers strictly define what they believe to be a crossroads. For some in an urban environment, only a crossroads with a stoplight counts and they use a small brush and pan to collect the detritus from the paving. Others go to a park's dirt-path crossing or prefer a place where a road and a railroad cross. Crossroads associated with nearby landmarks can carry those energies, such as Times Square for aspiring actors. Develop your own perspective.

Gather dirt from the corners and center of the crossroads while praying to the spirit of the location that it be strong in the material you are gathering. Pour a shot of whiskey in the center and leave three pennies as payment.

Crossroads dirt can be used to trace symbols on the altar, dust candles, or it may be added to oils, powders, and mojo hands. Baths and other spell remnants may be left or dispersed at a crossroads as well.

USING THE SEAL OF THE 72 NAMES OF GOD

It is believed that it was by the 72 names of the Hebrew God that the Biblical figure Moses had the power to part the Red Sea, granting passage for the fleeing Israelites. You can print out or draw this seal and burn it to ashes to add to Road Opener supplies, or write upon it as a petition paper. Anoint the seal with Road Opener or Moses Oil.

MAINTENANCE: HOW OFTEN SHOULD YOU CLEANSE?

Just as with mundane cleaning, there is no one spiritual bath, foot-wash, or house-cleaning that will keep you forever sparkly-bright. Every person's cleansing schedule will be different, so be aware of these variables:

- **Environment:** If your environment is chronically unclean or gets re-messed up due to a bad family or bad neighbourhood, cleanse weekly.
- **Sensitivity:** If your stability is easily capsized because you are naturally more open to influences than most people, cleanse every Sunday.
- **Weakness:** If you feel weak due to longstanding or generational curses, cleanse when needed, but increase the intervals as you build up strength.
- **Illness:** If you have a physical or mental illness that lowers your resistance, coordinate your cleanings with your medical treatments.

If you feel strong and only wish to perform regular maintenance cleansing, you may select one or more timing options from the list below:

- **Once a week:** Sunday mornings are recommended for taking personal cleansing baths, especially if you recite scriptural prayers as you bathe.
- **Once a month:** Choose any auspicious date or easy weekend day.
- **First day of the month:** This is done no matter when it falls in the week.
- **The day after the last day of a woman's period:** This is a traditional time for women to cleanse the body and refresh the senses.
- **The change of the moon:** About four days after the new moon or dark of the moon, a thin crescent is sighted low in the west at sunset; called the change of the moon, it marks the start of a new lunar month.
- **Every quarter year:** Observing the change of seasons at the solstices and the equinoxes with a house-cleaning is an old custom.
- **New Year's Eve or Day:** The first day of the year (at midnight or, in some cultures, at dawn) is a time of rituals; begin them by cleaning.
- **Your birthday:** There is no better way to begin your own personal new year than with a cleansing and self-blessing spiritual bath.
- **After a traumatic or distressing life event:** After a death, a divorce, the loss of a job, or the breakup of a friendship, bathe to mark a new start.
- **Upon moving into a new home:** Use a brand new broom and Chinese Wash to cleanse your new house or apartment before moving into it.

DEVELOPING RELATIONSHIPS WITH HELPING SPIRITS

It is the responsibility of all human beings to develop relationships with their Helping Spirits — those entities that innately walk with us and are here to help us understand and fulfill our soul's purpose. These include Ancestor Helping Spirits whose medicine is reflected in our talents, skills, and personas as well as guides appearing in a wide variety of forms, from animals to cosmic beings.

Getting to know one's Helping Spirits can begin with simple meditation techniques, such as closing your eyes and imagining yourself to be in a personal place of power such as a spot in nature. In such a visualization, you can use your inner senses of sight, sound, and touch to viscerally explore the landscape. When ready, call in one of your Helping Spirits and ask them to step forward. Experience them exactly the way they present themselves and ask them what name it best serves for you to call them. You can ask them questions about the nature of their relationship with you, ways in which they can help you, steps you can take to cultivate the connection, including proper offerings that they may prefer. They may speak to you in symbolic language, perform spontaneous healing acts, or otherwise communicate with you. When finished, express gratitude and gently bring yourself back to normal waking consciousness, writing down your experiences in a dedicated journal whether or not you grasp their full meaning. You may find that a white candle anointed with Spirit Guide or Clarity Oil can aid you, as can the burning of Althæa Leaf or Root and Frankincense. The veil between our world and theirs is so thin as to be non-existent and little is needed to make contact.

Helping Spirits can also be asked to appear in dreams, or may do so of their own accord if they feel that their presence is appropriate or beneficial. Techniques for prophetic dreaming can be employed with ease, such as anointing oneself with oils or bathing in suitable condition baths before sleep, though dedicated effort might be necessary for those who are inexperienced in receiving information via such states. Spending time in spaces devoted to honing these connections, such as Ancestor altars, is yet another popular way that folks invite their guides into their homes and lives.

If, for any reason, you should feel concerned that less-than-trustworthy spirits have been attracted, you can command them to tell their True Name in the name of Jesus Christ, or in the name of another heavenly Hoy Power with whom you have a positive relationship.

DEVELOPING RELATIONSHIPS WITH ANCESTORS

Today, many urban people are cut off from the practices their own Ancestors maintained to forge a connection to their forebears, but in the United States, the 19th century Spiritualist churches and the 20th century Spiritual Church Movement founded by Mother Leafy Anderson of Wisconsin reinvigorated African styles of Ancestor veneration in the diaspora. Simultaneously, the work of Allan Kardec, founder of Spiritism in 19th century France, provided a new spiritual methodology for works of mediumship that rapidly spread throughout Latin America and the Caribbean under the name Espiritismo. The techniques Kardec espoused helped to fill the gaps in ancestral reverence for African peoples who'd been physically displaced from the lands in which their dead were buried, forming a tradition that grew in parallel alongside such religions as Lucumí or Santería in Cuba.

HOW TO BUILD AN ANCESTOR ALTAR

In Spiritualism and Spiritism, both blood Ancestors and other spirit guides are honoured, with an emphasis on cleanliness and sweetness. An Ancestor altar (or boveda in Espiritismo) can be made by draping a white cloth over a dresser or a high shelf and arranging either six or eight long-stemmed glasses of water in an arc or circle with one slightly taller glass of water in the center. A drop of sweet-smelling perfume like Florida Water may be added to each glass and a white candle is lit as an offering of light to the spirits. Christian symbols such as crosses and crucifixes are common, but the important thing is to appeal to the sensibilities of your forebears. An Ancestor altar can also be as simple as one glass of water and a white candle set up in a clean space.

In African American Spiritualism, photos of both dead and living family may be displayed, so that the dead watch over their descendants, but in Latin America, it is traditional to ensure that no photos of the living are present.

Offerings such as coffee, tea, tobacco, candy, alcohol, flowers, and food may placed on the altar and incense burned as well. It is considered wise to offer items that the deceased who are represented on the altar preferred while they were alive. Generally, food and beverage offerings are left for a few days before being disposed of conventionally or at a place in nature.

Ancestor reverence is a highly personal affair, so these are not rules, only suggestions. Your truths will be based in your culture and in the experiences of ancestral contact you yourself have, both at the altar and elsewhere in life.

PLACEMENT OF THE ANCESTOR ALTAR IN THE HOME

Both cultural and personal choices inform the placement of ancestral altars. Some say that they should never be erected in the bedroom due to issues of sexual propriety. Others feel no such modesty and set theirs on the bedroom vanity or dresser. Some say that the kitchen is best because the dead want to be included in the daily conversations and activities of descendants. Others prefer the inviting formality of the living room fireplace mantelpiece.

TENDING TO THE ANCESTOR ALTAR

Many folks tend their Ancestor altar once a week, refreshing the water glasses, replacing food and offerings, putting out new candles, and spending time in meditation with their Ancestors by sitting before the altar after giving prayers of thanks and making requests. Others tend the altar daily.

An Ancestor altar is almost universally regarded as a "non-working" altar. Spells are not performed here, even in situations where ancestral aid is called upon. Rather, it is a place to commune and connect. However, in the Espiritismo tradition, you may cleanse yourself by verbally petitioning your dead relatives to help while running your hands down your body through your auric field and flicking energetic debris toward the altar. A splash of a perfume like Florida Water, Kolonia 1800, or Siete Machos on the hands before cleansing in this manner is traditional.

MEDIUMSHIP AT THE ANCESTOR ALTAR

Many people consider their Ancestors and personal spirit guides to be their primary source for gaining wisdom and clarity, as well as their first line of defense against attack. If you seeks to hone your mediumship abilities, then time spent at your Ancestor altar can be of great help as well. After giving offerings and expressing gratitude, pray sincerely from the heart for guidance, wisdom, and clarity. Then, sit in silence before the altar for at least 15 minutes and, afterwards, record your impressions. These may be images, thoughts, or words that came to mind during the meditation.

Performing this activity at least once a week can have a tremendous effect on your intuitive abilities and the grace with which you move through life. If you "don't experience anything," continue anyway. The dead may make their messages known in dreams or in everyday signs and omens. Many psychic readers attribute their intuitive insight to the aide of their Ancestors and many root doctors believe their help is integral to the potency of their work.

HOW TO PERFORM AN ANCESTRAL ELEVATION

Ancestral Elevation is a nine-day Spiritist rite performed to help spirits of the dead progress in their evolution. Through intercession and words of comfort and relief, this work can help transport the departed from the physical plane to the ancestral realms, or from a non-physical plane to an even "higher" realm, which can benefit the living as well.

Ancestral Elevation can be performed for one or more specific Ancestors, for all of one's Ancestors who need it, and even for spirits of the dead who are not biologically related to the practitioner. It is a truly malleable rite whose components can be altered according to the tastes and traditions important to the spirits of the dead who are being elevated, such as the inclusion of prayers from the religions they practiced when alive.

For this work you will need a white altar cloth, one large (or nine small) white candles, eight sturdy books or bricks, and a glass of clean water. Pleasant-smelling incense is a nice addition. Commercial self-lighting condition incenses such as Blessing, Healing, and Spirit Guide are good; alternatively, you can burn resins and herbs like Frankincense, Myrrh, and Althæa Root chips on a self-lighting charcoal disk. If Native Americans are among the Ancestors, Tobacco, Sweet Grass, or Indian Spirit Guide Incense may be used as well. You may dress your white candle(s) with one or more oils that speak to the energies of blessing, healing, peace, or love uncrossing.

First, create an altar by spreading the white cloth on a clean surface with the glass of water at the center atop the cloth. You may add white flowers to the altar or religious items that would be comforting to the souls of the dead you are elevating, for example, draping a rosary over the glass of water for souls who were Catholic while alive. If the rite is being performed for photos of the deceased are available, you may include them on the altar while ensuring that no photos of the living are present.

Place a white candle on the altar and light it along with your incense, burning it both as an offering to any benevolent spirits who arrive to offer aid and as a comfort to the souls of the dead whom you are elevating.

You may find the following words to be an inspiration:

"I call upon my Ancestral Helping Spirits — those who lived well, died well, made it through the Veil, and chose to accompany me in this lifetime. I call out to you who bring all that is beautiful, true, and just into my life. Be here now to protect me and to aid me in the elevation of these souls this day [or night]."

You may now choose to call out to any other helpful spirits with whom you have a strong relationship as well as any benevolent spirits who wish to aid in providing comfort and elevation to the souls you are assisting. Feel their presence around you.

"I call out to [name the specific spirits, or use a generic term, such as 'my unresolved dead'] to be here now. Partake of this cool, clear water. May it quench your thirst. Partake of this incense. May it bring you peace and comfort. Partake of this candle flame. May it light your way now and forever. I remember you and I offer you light, love, and progress."

The more passion and energy you put into these words, the better. Emit the energies of love and remembrance toward the souls you are elevating. Each word is an offering. You may feel inspired to improvise or make gestures, for example, raising your hands to symbolize elevation.

"Your grief is known, [insert names], and you are not forgotten. You are remembered, [insert names], and the time of grieving is now at an end. The time of sorrow is over. Now is the time for celebration and joy, for you are loved and remembered unto the Great Fabric. Whatever you are holding on to, let it go. Whatever happened during your lifetime — all is forgiven. All is forgiven and you are remembered and loved. Be elevated. Be elevated. Be elevated. It is for the good of all."

Prayerfully ask your Guiding Spirits to aid in helping these souls let go of what is holding them back. At this time, you may offer up traditional prayers or songs that would be comforting to the Ancestors you are elevating., perhaps scriptures such as Psalms 23, songs like "Amazing Grace," prayers such as the Our Father. Imagine your voice as a sound bridge connecting these souls from the plane they are on the plane it would best serve them to get to, as you say these words:

"If there are any souls that are ready and able to be moved on, I ask the benevolent spirits accompanying me in this rite to take them there now."

Then thank your Helping Spirits for their protection and aid in elevating the souls you are assisting, and snuff out your candle.

The next day, dismantle the altar and place a second book or brick on the clean surface, and drape the white cloth over it. Reassemble your altar on top of this with a glass of fresh, clean water. Perform the service again, each day adding a book or brick to the stack and reassembling the altar setup on top of it. At the end of nine days, you may choose to perform divination on the effects of your work.

CONSIDERATIONS IN ANCESTOR PRACTICE

Because I have seen harmful presences and patterns left by the unresolved ancestral dead in the lives of my clients, I personally call upon "my Ancestral Helping Spirits — those who lived well and died well, made it through the Veil, and chose to accompany me in this lifetime" rather than calling on the Ancestors in general. This ensures that I am bringing in only those who resolved their lives before or after death, and not summoning ghosts or the restless dead who seek to hijack the living to fix their own unresolved lives.

The question of whom to honour when instances of familial abuse have occurred is a sensitive one. I am of the opinion that you should not invite to your altar anyone you would not invite into your home, and that healing needs to take place on both sides of the veil between life and death before some Ancestors and their descendants are ready to work together as a team.

Ancestral concerns can manifest as ghostly hauntings by a forebear who is burdensome and demanding. Some who practice Ancestor reverence may even honour such spirits at an altar, believing that the drama, neediness, and antics come with the territory, but this is not so. Such spirits may benefit you in some ways, but harm you in others. I recommend calling on Ancestors who are more elevated or mature for help in dealing with them.

Ancestral issues can also appear as mental and emotional patterns and habits that seem insurmountable despite the work someone has done to heal themselves and resolve the issue. These are generally deeper and require more effort than the above as the Ancestor might not be easily accessible though the pattern they generated in their family line is present.

It is not uncommon for folks to make payment at a Catholic Church to have a mass said for one or more deceased relatives or loved ones to help accomplish what the above Spiritist-style rite of Ancestral Elevation aims.

It is less common, but quite effective, to set lights for the progress of Ancestors whose energies are hindering the living. Blessing, Healing, and Uncrossing vigil lights are all good options here, and you can set them yourself or hire a qualified rootworker or Spiritualist to set them for you.

CONJUREMAN ALI'S ANCESTRAL CURSE REMOVAL

To break the hold of a generational curse, work an Uncrossing Spell Kit while reciting 1 Chronicles 1:1-28 from Adam through the sons of Abraham, followed by a recitation of the family's names, going seven generations back, if possible, followed by the entirety of Psalms 25.

DEVELOPING RELATIONSHIPS WITH ANGELS AND SAINTS

Folk magic is an assertion of personal power in the face of adversity, but few rootworkers would say that they act alone in their work, instead giving the glory to God, their Ancestors, and other guides in gratitude for both their well-being and their achievements in remediating concerns.

Though the Southern Baptist foundations of hoodoo put the Biblical God front and center for many practitioners, as the tradition gains traction worldwide, many different varied and fluid understandings of Divinity have found conjure-style workings and petitions placed on altars before them. Contrastingly, individuals who may not have been previously inclined to step outside of their religious or cultural bubbles have come to do so after finding resonance with entities popular amongst other spiritworkers they've encountered, or for sheer sake of efficacy in times of need and desire.

It is important to remember hoodoo's origins and the power that the tradition says exists in the name of Jesus Christ, in the proclamation of his Blood, and in the Bible as a book of wisdom, guidance, and spiritual power. This need not occlude an eye toward eclecticism, which is more than helpful for any spiritual practitioner working on the world stage as a tremendous variety of helpful and benevolent spirits do exist and walk alongside everyday folks toward aiding them in fulfillment of their soul's purpose. As a contemporary spiritual doctor, being able to discern and speak to the cosmology that one is encountering may indeed be a new-fangled sign of the times, but it is a skill that does more than benefit a client's comfort level. It helps to ensure the preservation and remembrance of the many spiritual traditions that are the building blocks of our world. Hoodoo's worldwide popularity and accessibility place it in a unique position that helps folks the world over tap into their own cultural heritages as it interfaces with time periods and landscapes far from home.

Most seasoned spiritual practitioners have strong personal relationships with working spirits whom they can call upon for aid on behalf of themselves and others. I've included in the following pages introductions to some spirits that are worked with amongst contemporary practitioners of Catholic and Folk Catholic styles of hoodoo. Due to their visibility and popularity, they are generally accessible and available to those who approach them with a sincere heart, and have been known to move mountains in times of both mundane and spiritual emergency.

ARCHANGEL MICHAEL

One of the most beloved spirits among magical practitioners, the Jewish Archangel Michael — also known in other religious communities as Mikail, Mikhail, Saint Michael the Archangel, and San Miguel — is a Biblical figure often called upon to protect those who are under attack by adversaries, whether spirit or human. Depicted as a sword-bearing winged man subduing a dragon, a demon, or the Devil over the flaming pit of Hell, he is the patron of law enforcement agents, and of all who face danger.

Archangel Michael can be petitioned with heartfelt prayers and with red candles. Medallions bearing his visage may be anointed with oils bearing his name and worn by those who seek refuge under him. Many folk magicians and spirit mediums keep a statue of Archangel Michael in their homes, and seek his supplementary aid in larger magical workings. but some say that his divine light is so bright that it outshines that of other helpful spirits in his vicinity and they prefer to keep his statue away from their main altar spaces, standing him by the front or back door as a ward against harmful intruders.

Holy cards with an image of Michael on the front and a prayer on the back may be inserted into wallets or stitched into the garments of beloved family members by prayerful caregivers. In Lousiana, Saint Michael cards are glued or stitched to house-protection packets containing Grains of Paradise seeds.

HOW TO MAKE A SAINT MICHAEL AMPARO

An amparo is a Latin America protection charm. Those who work with the Mexican spirit Santa Muerte (Holy Death) often make an amparo with Saint Michael or Saint Cyprian to help subdue Death's more demanding aspects.

Take two Saint Michael holy cards and lay them next to one another, both face-down. Place a photo of the person for whom you seek protection on top of one of the prayer cards. Anoint the four corners and the center of the photo with Archangel Michael Oil or Fiery Wall of Protection Oil. Take the second card and place it over the photo so that the image of Saint Michael is facing outwards on both sides, guarding from the front and back. Take a red or white string and wrap the holy cards and photo together so that the string forms a cross on both sides. Prayerfully call out to Archangel Saint Michael to protect the individual whose photo is inside. A white or a red candle dressed with either of the two named oils can be burned on top of the amparo before it is given to the person for whom it has been crafted.

ARCHANGEL RAPHAEL

Archangel Raphael, whose name means "God heals," is the patron of fishermen, travellers, and those who work in the healing arts, including doctors, nurses, and spiritworkers. His remarkable story is told in the Jewish apocryphal Book of Tobit. In Islam he is known as Israfil. He has been declared a Saint by the Catholic Church, so statues and vigil candles depicting him as Saint Raphael the Archangel or San Rafael are easily found, and may be used in works of devotion and petition, including the popular nine-day novena prayer. Two herbs associated with him are Althæa and Angelica: Althæa means "healer" in Greek, and Angelica means "angel."

Like all archangels, Raphael is accessible to everyone and requires no offerings for his aid. In addition to healing physical, mental, and emotional afflictions, he will remove demonic spirits that are attached to a person or place. He is a deft clearer of spaces that are besieged by negative energies.

Although he is an archangel, those who are not Jewish generally petition him in the same way that they would work with a sainted human being; for example, medallions with his image on them can be anointed or prayed over and worn by those afflicted with ailments, or they may be sewn onto cloth pouches filled with herbs, roots, and curios that aid in bringing healing and encouraging wholeness while he is petitioned to bless the talisman. You may brew a tea of Althæa and Angelica, add a few drops of Archangel Raphael Oil or Healing Oil, and pour this into the floor wash used to clean a sickroom as you ask for his help. People and rooms may also be smoked with Archangel Raphael incense if his assistance is desired.

A PRAYER TO ARCHANGEL RAPHAEL

Blessed Saint Raphael, Archangel,
We beseech you to help us in all our needs and trials of this life.
As you, through the power of God, restored sight to Tobit,
And as you gave guidance to young Tobias,
And as you drove the demon Asmodeus away from Sarah,
We humbly seek your aid and intercession,
That our souls may be healed,
Our bodies protected from all ills
And that through divine grace we may be fit
To dwell in the eternal Glory of God in Heaven. Amen.

SAINT CYPRIAN OF ANTIOCH

Legend and lore tell us that the human Saint Cyprian of Antioch was an extremely adept magician, who worked with demons in the spiritually sorcerous style of Europe and North Africa during the late 3rd century. When his spell-casting to ruin the virginity of a young Christian woman named Justina failed three times in the face of her faith, he made the sign of the cross, renounced his ways, converted to Christianity, and eventually became the renowned Bishop of Antioch. Both he and Justina were martyred under the persecution of Diocletian in an area that is now part of Turkey.

Due to lack of historical evidence regarding his existence, the Catholic Church has removed his feast day from its official calendar; however, he remains a popular figure with occultists around the globe, providing a link between church ritual, the grimoire tradition, and folk magical practices. He is the patron of spiritworkers, sorcerers, conjure doctors, and all who practice the magical arts — in fact "Cyprianus" is a popular term for a grimoire in Scandinavian folk magic. Saint Cyprian spiritual supplies are easy to find, but you may also use Master Key or Black Arts products when petitioning him.

Saint Cyprian's devotees seek his aid for skill in the dark arts and as a personal guide who encourages self-mastery under his tutelage. He is known for protection from evil, exorcism of harmful beings, removal of curses and the evil eye, and facilitating spirit contact between the living, the dead, and beings that are neither.

PRAYER TO SAINT CYPRIAN OF ANTIOCH
(Make the sign of the cross where + is written):
Saint Cyprian of Antioch, I beseech you
    that those bound by evil spirits and wicked sorceries be unbound. +
I beseech you to shatter all bewitchments and oppressions. +
Save us from the dominion of the wild beasts. +
Saint Cyprian, preserve us from all evil sorceries, spirits,
    and malicious arts. +
Guard us in thought, action, and feeling. +
Throw into confusion the wicked ones who seek our lives. +
Confound them with your power. +
Holy Saint Cyprian I beseech you to be our guard and saviour. +
By your power may we triumph forever more. Amen. +

SAINT EXPEDITE: PATRON OF RAPID SOLUTIONS

This Roman centurion who became a Catholic Saint is a mystery. His popularity is greatest in Portugal, Spain, and Louisiana. Bearing a cross with "hodi," the Latin word for "today," on it while subduing a crow with a banner in its beak that reads "cras" ("tomorrow" in Latin), he is called martyr, protector, noble Roman youth, and Patron Saint of Procrastinators.

Turned to in times of financial need and "quality of life" emergencies, he is also called upon to work fast miracles in other areas of life, including love, gambling, legal matters, and works of harm.

Nearly as famous as Saint Expedite himself is the relatively strict protocol which folks say must be adhered to if one seeks to retain what has been gained through his intercession. As a soldier, he is used to taking orders, and works contractually, and it is nearly impossible to come by information regarding him without the warning that what he gives can be taken back if what was promised to him has been forgotten or withheld. Traditionally he is said to accept a slice of pound cake, coffee, red carnations or roses, red wine, red candles, silver dimes, and public praise for his achievements.

PETITIONING SAINT EXPEDITE

On a Wednesday, arrange a red candle, a glass of clean water, and a statue or print image of Saint Expedite on an altar in a triangle, with the candle at the back apex, the water at front-left, and the image at front-right. Dress the candle with Saint Expedite Oil or Fast Luck Oil. Light the candle and knock on the altar surface while calling Saint Expedite's name aloud. A popular prayer to him said in times of financial emergency or other crisis reads:

Our dear martyr and protector, Saint Expedite,
You who know what is necessary and what is urgently needed.
I beg you to intercede before the Holy Trinity,
That by your grace my request will be granted.
(Clearly express your needs and ask him to find a way to fulfill them.)
May I receive your blessings and favours.
In the name of our Lord Jesus Christ, Amen.

Offer fresh flowers to the Saint following his intercession on your behalf. They can be kept on the home or left at a church. It is important to remember that payment is made to Saint Expedite after he has come to your aid.

SAINT JUDE: HOPE OF THE HOPELESS

One of Jesus's apostles, known as the "Patron of Lost Causes and Hopeless Cases," Saint Jude is petitioned for relief in desperate situations. Being the saint most associated with making possible the seemingly impossible, his help often arrives in the final moment. Petitioners often make a vow to publish their gratitude for Saint Jude's help in a public forum, and personals columns of newspapers far and wide as well as internet forums carry brief statements of thanks to the saint as a testament to his aide for all to see. Use Saint Jude, Healing, or other appropriate spiritual supplies when petitioning him.

PRAYER TO SAINT JUDE
A suggested prayer to the saint in times of dire health reads as follows:
Dear Apostle and Martyr for Christ,
You left us an Epistle in the New Testament.
With good reason many invoke you when illness is at a desperate stage.
We now recommend to your kindness (name) who is in critical condition.
May the cure of this patient increase (his / her) faith and love
For the Lord of Life, for the glory of our merciful God. Amen.

DR. JOSE GREGORGIO HERNANDEZ

Dr. Jose Gregorio Hernandez (1864 - 1919) was a Venezuelan physician and professor of medicine who devoted himself to a life of charity by offering free health services to the poor. Known as "The Servant of God," he also received religious training, as he felt called to a spiritual ministry. He was killed in a traffic accident at the age of 54, while delivering medicine to a patient, but miracles associated with him soon followed and, at the time of this writing, he is in on his way to being canonized by the Catholic Church.

Dr. Hernandez is most often petitioned when a proper diagnosis or a qualified medical practitioner is sought. Medical students also ask his help when preparing for tests, and those who are under hospital care or in surgery may find his intercession on their behalf to be a tremendous boon in their treatment and recovery.

Prayer cards, novena candles, and Dr. Hernandez spiritual supplies bearing his image are easily found. If he grants a petition, financial contributions given in his name to those in need of medical help are a welcome offering.

SAN SIMÓN MAXIMON

An ancient Mayan god named "Maam" ("Grandfather" in Mayan), rejected by the Catholic Church and syncretized with Judas Iscariot, Maximon or San Simón is honoured most in his homeland, Guatemala. In the late 20th century, Central American immigrants brought him to the United States and he is now found on the altars of eclectic hoodoo practitioners.

Known as "Hermano" ("brother" in Spanish), and also as Champion of the Hopeless, his seemingly imposing nature and love of vice stand in sharp contrast to his affable and often comical nature. Statues generally depict Hermano Simón as a seated older man holding a staff and wearing a wide-brimmed hat. His second most common manifestation is as an effigy covered in scarves and ties who wears a pair of sunglasses just above a bandana covering the bottom half of his face. Effigies are an important part of his worship, as are the cigars and cigarettes placed in the holes fashioned to be his mouth. Tobacco is of tremendous importance to him and traditional prayers cite tortillas, alcohol (especially aguardiente), sausage fruits, sausages, and copal incense as favourites as well. Maximon or San Simón spiritual supplies such as candles, statuary, and oils are readily available.

An "all-purpose" saint petitioned for protection, removal of witchcraft, attracting a lover, and ensuring the good health and the welfare of adults and children, he is possibly most well-known for his aid in money and business matters for which green and blue candles are lit before his image along with prayers and offerings. A cigarette and strong faith seem to be the most important factors in attracting his favour but, somewhat ironically, this generosity extends to his willingness to help in matters of ending addiction to both nicotine and alcohol — and possibly other substances, if belief in his ability to aid is of proper intensity.

PETITIONING MAXIMON FOR AN END TO ADDICTIONS

To petition San Simón for help in bringing an end to substance addiction, light a purple glass-encased candle before his image and offer him some Tobacco in the form of a cigarette or cigar which can be lit and smoked a bit before him or pressed to the saint's lips in the image used, praying:

Oh mighty San Simón, I come to you.
Let your spirit help me in all actions and in any dangerous circumstances
I want you to perform the miracles that I request. (State request.) Amen.

HOW TO FIND THE RIGHT ROOT DOCTOR

Nowhere is the need for spiritual help more evident than in people's lives held siege by severe crossed conditions they have been unable to ameliorate themselves. If a reading or divination has indicated that you are crossed or under spiritual attack, but you feel unsure of your own ability to lift the curse or break the jinx, you may wish to seek a professional conjure doctor to assist you. I do not intend to discourage your personal practice of hoodoo, but to encourage you to seek out and get help, if needed, from those whose lives are defined by, and a testament to, the beauty and power of this work. Even after you have studied this book, it is okay to hire a helper, a teacher, someone to back up your work, or someone to handle your case from start to finish.

Although there is a popular belief that the most effective spells are those that are performed by the person who wants them done, specialists exist in the spiritual arts for a reason. Nearly every culture on earth recognizes the equivalent of being gifted for the work — a Black-American phrase signifying someone naturally talented in mysticism, seership, and magic — and gifted workers who operate ethical, conscientious practices are well worth what they charge. In addition to study under mentors, years of hands-on application, and hundreds of amassed case studies, these individuals have often cultivated strong bonds with spiritual entities that aid them in their work and they are committed to serving their clients and their communities.

It is unfortunate that unscrupulous individuals claiming to be helpful and knowledgeable exist alongside skilled and gifted ones, and that in today's world, finding ethical, effective, affordable spiritual help can feel like looking for a needle in a haystack. This truly should not be the case. Compassionate healers, workers, and teachers exist in every cultural tradition. Many can be found in the Association of Independent Readers and Rootworkers (AIRR), a directory founded in 2007 to promote ethical spiritual services to the public. All AIRR members are approved by accreditation and evaluation, each is trained in African-American folk magic, and most offer magical coaching for those who want to learn how to cast their own spells.

Find the directory of AIRR members online at:

ReadersandRootworkers.org

Learn the danger signs of cold readings, canned readings, fraudulent spiritual titles, and candle scams online at this web page:

LuckyMojo.com/blackgypsies.html

Here are some things to avoid when seeking a psychic or spellcaster:

- **Makes guarantees:** Can a lawyer guarantee that she will win your case? Can a surgeon guarantee to will heal you? The best people in any field can still only do the best they can. Nothing in life is guaranteed.
- **Claims to solve all your problems:** No psychic, shaman, spell-caster, mambo, babalawo, tata, sorceresss, or witch can solve all of your life problems with one spell. Beware of grandiose claims.
- **Asks nothing of you but money:** Authentic root doctors generally ask clients to bathe, pray, and cleanse their homes to back up the work. They may send you spiritual supplies by mail or give you a shopping list of items to purchase locally or online so that you will have what you need to do your part. A spell-caster who does not ask you to back up the work may be selling you imaginary spells, so go ahead and ask for altar photos — but be aware that fake workers copy online altar photos from genuine practitioners to use as "proof" that they are working for you.
- **Offers 24-hour love returns and reconciliations:** If a worker claims to reconcile lovers in 24 hours, do not deal with that person for any reason. Spiritual repair of relationships takes time, especially when hard feelings are still present. Honest love-workers may limit the conditions under which they will take a job, request clients to send personal concerns, and prescribe back-up work for clients to perform. They can usually give you a timeline for their work; it will be neither 24 hours nor open-ended.
- **Has the most powerful spells:** The person who claims to be "the most powerful spell-caster" usually isn't. The most effective, clear spiritworkers I know are also deeply humble, knowing that unseen hands aid their work and that their efficacy is at least partly an outgrowth of the relationship they have with the spirit world.
- **Uses scare tactics:** If a psychic or spiritworker threatens you with a life of hopelessness or tells you that he or she is the only person who can help you, RUN — don't walk — away. Such a worker is lying to you and trying to frighten you into giving up your power (and your wallet). You can take your own steps toward wholeness, well-being, and goal achievement. Anyone who tells you otherwise only intends to harm you.
- **Offers $5.00 specials:** I've never met a psychic offering $5.00 specials who didn't give canned or rote readings meant to lure clients in with generalities and hook them with charismatic tactics. Don't take the bait.

When seeking a spiritual or magical help, be sure to look for:

- **Empowerment:** I've never seen a circumstance in my readings where there wasn't an opportunity to empower my client. In fact, no such circumstance in the Universe exists. If a reading leaves you feeling disempowered, reclaim your power immediately and take a cleansing bath. A light at the end of the tunnel can be conjured out of even the most crossed of conditions, without you becoming dependent on the worker who has read for you. Indeed, hiring spiritual help should feel hopeful and empowering, not draining or terrifying, no matter what your need. If you are told "It always gets worse before it gets better," get away.
- **Honesty and integrity:** Forget the men and women of mystery who are too big and bad to reveal who they are. The most effective psychics and practitioners I know tell it plainly. Some of them may use pseudonyms or titles, especially in alignment with the tradition or culture their work is borne from, but they're glad to express who they are because their work is an outgrowth of their very real lives and experiences.
- **Clear communication guidelines:** If you hire someone to remediate a condition, expect a timeline regarding when the work will start and end, as well as what the communication expectations are. When would be a good time to check in about the work? What modes of communication are best? How long should it take for a response? Knowing the answers to these questions ahead of time will help you avoid a lot of frustration.
- **Custom work:** The answer to a money problem isn't always a money drawing spell and not every type of cleansing is for every type of malady. A good worker will tailor the job to suit your needs. This should include awareness of any medical or allergy issues you may have, especially if home baths or in-person cleansing rites are prescribed.
- **A desire to educate:** From podcasts and radio shows to teleseminars, blogs, Facebook groups, workshops, and books, most online readers share their thoughts, philosophies, and experiences with the world. Not every effective spiritworker has access to the internet, but a desire for you to understand the basis of the work should be evident.
- **Willingness to refer:** Just as it would be unethical for a pediatrician not to recommend a podiatrist if the root of a problem is in the feet, so is it only ethical for a spiritworker who knows that he or she cannot help you to refer you to someone who can.

SPIRITUAL AND SOCIAL RESOURCES

- **Modest Needs Foundation: ModestNeeds.org**
This non-profit organization works to responsibly provide short-term financial assistance to individuals and families in temporary crisis who are working and live just above the poverty level.
- **Law Help: LawHelp.org**
Help for people of low and moderate incomes find free legal aid programs in their communities, answers to questions about their legal rights and forms to help them with their legal problems.
- **Crystal Silence League: CrystalSilenceLeague.org**
Founded in 1919 to distribute affirmative prayer to all, their web site exists for the posting of prayers to be prayed over by dedicated members around the world. "Prayer is always free at the Crystal Silence League."
- **Hoodoo Psychics: HoodooPsychics.com**
This psychic line offers readings, but with a BIG difference: All the readers are also rootworkers, so you can pay by the minute for spell-casting suggestions or get a check reading on your own spell work.
- **The Focusing Institute: Focusing.org**
This not-for-profit organization brings self-help skills to the public. An affordable resource, it puts you in touch with your felt sense, intuition, and body-wisdom, to understand what you are truly feeling and wanting.
- **Sylvia Rivera Law Project: SPLP.org**
SRLP works to guarantee that all people are free to self-determine their gender identity and expression, regardless of income or race, and without facing harassment, violence, or discrimination.

Crisis Counseling Phone Numbers (USA)

Abused Children	1-800-422-4453
AIDS - National AIDS Hotline	1-800-232-4636
Alcoholism - Alcohol Helpline	1-800-622-2255
Domestic Violence Hotline	1-800-799-SAFE
Gay and Trans Youth Crisis Hotline	1-866-488-7386
Missing Children	1-800-USA-KIDS
Planned Parenthood	1-800-230-PLAN
Sexual Assault Hotline	1-800-656-HOPE
Suicide Prevention Lifeline	1-800-273-8255

Frequently Asked Questions

The Lucky Mojo Forum was begun in 2008. Averaging 60 posts per day, it is an online community in which questions are answered daily with regards to the practice of hoodoo and the use of Lucky Mojo spiritual supplies. The Forum is open to all, and anyone can join and ask questions.

The Lucky Mojo Forum can be accessed online at

Forum.LuckyMojo.com

Answers to questions, be they in the form of advice, encouragement, clarification, or spell suggestions, are provided by both forum members and a dedicated team of moderators, all of whom are graduates of catherine yronwode's Hoodoo Rootwork Correspondence Course.

Read more about the Hoodoo Rootwork Correspondence Course at

LuckyMojo.com/mojocourse.html

The Frequently Asked Questions — and answers — that follow have been selected form a voluminous body of information at the Forum regarding hoodoo uncrossing and jinx-breaking practices. The record contained in the following pages is intended to complete and augment the information included in the preceding pages. Here you will find answers to some of the most commonly asked questions in the Forum regarding uncrossing, protection, healing, money, success, and spirituality.

When reading the answers to the questions provided, note that the usernames followed by an (M) are people who are or were at one time Forum moderators. Those marked (M, AIRR) are moderators who are also in professional practice and members of the Association of Independent Readers and Rootworkers:

Miss Aida	**ConjureMan Ali**
Miss Bri	**Miss Michaele**
catherine yronwode	**Miss Phoenix**

These folks and other AIRR members can be reached for personal readings, rootwork, magical coaching, custom spell-casting, and related professional services at the AIRR web site:

ReadersAndRootworkers.org

• Should cleansing baths be taken before and after all spell-work?

Before and after doing a spell, should I cleanse myself?
— Bella06

Cleanse yourself before starting spell work. Use Chinese Wash or Van Van.

Don't cleanse after using supplies for drawing, like Love Me, Fast Luck, Healing, Prosperity, House Blessing, Wealthy Way, Look Me Over, Lucky Number, or Crown of Success. You want to keep what you did on you.

Don't cleanse after spells of removal, reversal, or protection with products like Jinx Killer, Uncrossing, Fiery Wall of Protection, or Reversing, because such a spell is also a cleansing trick, so cleansing would be redundant.

Do clean up after negative tricks with Hot Foot, Destruction, Break-Up, Jinx, or Damnation products. The cleansing is to take off your own sin if, God forbid, you called down an unjust curse on the head of an innocent person.
— catherineyronwode (M, AIRR)

• How can I undo tricks laid in food?

My husband has been fed something in food to make him hate me and leave me. What should be my immediate steps to get rid of it?
— yukon2015

Go to HerbMagic.com and search for the word "uncross" or "uncrossing." Research which uncrossing herbs are safe to drink or use in cooking. Your husband was fed a spell, so he must eat or drink the spell-breaker.
— MissMichaele (M, AIRR)

• What should I do with candle remains?

Should I bury candle spell remains in my garden, put them under my bed, or leave them at a crossroads?
— silver_disc

Please, please, please, recycle your glass vigil light holders! Do not throw them away, do not bury them. Recycling or reusing them is the way to go.
— Miss Bri (M, AIRR)

• Can I take Cut and Clear or Black Walnut baths for others?

I am planning on doing the Black Walnut spell and a Cut and Clear spell on behalf of someone who was crossed in love. Can I take the baths myself, or must I have the person I am doing the work for take the baths?
— bluesky

Bathing by proxy, either on one's own body or by the bathing of dolls that are named to represent a client, is part of our tradition. It's just not all that easy — and the particular baths that you named are ones that most workers feel must be taken by the person who wishes to be cleansed.

It would take a very experienced and powerfully focused professional to take a bath for another person by proxy to break a love obsession — and even then, i doubt it would be half as effective as getting the person to do the work for him or her self, even if the person were half-scared and 16 years old.
— catherineyronwode (M, AIRR)

• How and why should I build an Ancestor altar?

How do I build an altar? What do I build an altar for? Am I silly for resonating so deeply with the idea of an Ancestor altar?
— TrynaKnowNGrow

Creating an Ancestor altar is not "silly." It is a basic form of altar work. My Ancestor altar holds things from my own bloodline, my husband's bloodline, deceased pets, and teachers and mentors who have passed who are not my blood but are my family of spirit. Also on it are deer bones, a black candle with a skull carved into it, and a stone from Avebury, a place of my spiritual ancestry. This eclectic Ancestor altar fits my life and it holds a place of honour in my home. When people see it they know exactly what it is.

Another kind of altar is one where you venerate spirits, angels, saints, or deities. It is customary to place statuary or offerings on such an altar.

You may also wish to build a working altar, where you will cast spells; it should have a fireproof surface if you intend to burn candles there.

I have written a book on this subject that may be of further help to you: **Hoodoo Shrines and Altars: Sacred Spaces in Rootwork and Conjure.**
— Miss Phoenix (M, AIRR)

• Can I use Block Buster for my wife's spiritual health?

My wife just changed her office at work and there are a lot of people with health problems. When she is near them she feels a burning in her head, pain to the stomach, and difficulty of concentration. I gave her Block Buster Oil to put around her desk and on her head and she is feeling better but at the end of the day, she is stll tired and full of bad energy. How can I help my wife?
— Magister 9

I do not think Block Buster Oil would be the way to go for something like this. To start I would get some Uncrossing products, particularly the Bath Crystals, to wash off anything that may be clinging to you both. Then follow that by anointing yourselves with Blessing Oil and Healing Oil and praying for your blessings. Finally, use either Fiery Wall of Protection or Protection products at her place of work to keep off any further negative conditions.
— Nathen / natstein (M)

• Which Catholic saints are petitioned for depression?

Which saint candle is best to burn for healing depression?
— lmlvr

There are several Catholic saint and hoodoo candles used for depression.
If the situation may benefit from a doctor's diagnosis and care, try Dr. Jose Gregorio Hernandez.
If the condition is longstanding and you are already consulting a doctor (people with serious depression should always be seen by a competent medical professional), then use Healing and Clarity candles.
If the depression stems from childhood abuse, use Saint Dymphna candles.
If the situation is a temporary one caused by sad situations, try Blessing.
If bad people or bad habits of your own have gotten you down, add Cast Off Evil or Jesus the King candles to your list.
For more energy, try Power, John the Conqueror, or Blessing candles.
For more motivation, try Saint Expedite, who gets things done in a hurry.
Finally, there is a full "Spell for Blessing a Depressed Person" here:
LuckyMojo.com/blessing.html
— catherineyronwode (M, AIRR)

• How can I lift a curse that was made and regretted?

A dear friend wants to unmake a curse she cast on her mother when she was a teen. The curse was "to die of a long slow painful death." Her mother has lacked vitality for a while.
— gg_aleksandr_999

Make a clay doll. Cleanse it for 13 days in 13 Herb Bath while reciting Psalms 37, smoke it each day in Uncrossing Incense, and anoint it all over with Uncrossing Oil. Keep it wrapped up in a white cloth with protection herbs. Then perform a candle spell with three Uncrossing vigil lights in a triangle for the Past, Present, and Future, placing the doll in the middle.
— Miss Aida (M, AIRR)

• Can spells take a while because your faith is being tested?

Can spells take a long time to work for the purpose of testing your faith?
— K54

I think that some spells have tested my faith. Other spells, I think, just taught me to be more realistic because some situations will not manifest in a month. I've learned to trust myself, and to let go of certain situations.
— starssinthesky7 (M)

• What should I do for nighttime protection?

Which herbs, oils, candles, etc. will help with my nighttime protection?
— Guided09

Sprinkle salt in the four corners of your house, room, or bed while calling down protection. Using Fiery Wall of Protection products is not as simple as sprinkling salt, but it literally will create a barrier that keeps your enemy at bay. You can also mix Agrimony, Verbena, and Dragon's Blood and burn that in your house to purify it and send back dark workings, or you can sprinkle your house with Rue tea. Finally, you can make or purchase a protective mojo hand to carry with you or keep under your mattress.
— ConjureMan Ali (M, AIRR)

• How can I cleanse and uncross my relationship?

My boyfriend have been together for years and we don't even live together and I really want to. After having a conversation with him last night I realized that something needs to be done to uncross our relationship first.

We don't trust each other because of stupid mistakes we've made in the past. We have both been involved with other people while we were together, but now neither one of us is cheating. We really want to be together but we need some blessing in our relationship. I want us to feel like we felt in the beginning. I'm thinking about doing a cleansing, but I don't want to undo the love work that I'm doing and that I have already done.

If I do a cleansing will it undo my love work?

If not, then what kind of cleansing should I do?

How can I bless our relationship?

What can I do to increase our trust and faithfulness?

— financialsuccess2013

There are several ways you can approach this. I would first start by cleansing the bedroom or the place where the both of you sleep. Use Chinese Wash to clear out any negative energy or the energies of others that may be affecting the relationship. I would do this especially if you two sleep in the same bedroom most nights.

If he is open to the idea of a bath, it would be perfect for you two to cleanse in a bath such as 13 Herb Bath to knock off any bad luck that could be clinging to the relationship. If you have Healing Oil, then adding a few drops could be perfect for this situation. You do not need to tell him the reason for this bath. Just make it a loving time together.

Follow up the cleansing of the bedroom and the personal healing bath by using some Chuparrosa for honesty, Love Me for fidelity, or Fire of Love for passion. You may select the vigil candles, or use plain unmarked candles dressed with a blend of these three oils, or burn the incense all throughout the house — and let the LOVE come in!

Cleansing floor washes and baths will not "undo" any previous or ongoing love spells. If anything, cleaning yourselves and the bedroom should enhance your work. Just be clear in your intention while you are performing the cleansing. Good Luck!!

— ProphetAvery

Bibliography

ALI, ConjureMan. *Defending Against the Dark Arts*. Pamphlet. Missionary Independent Spiritual Church, 2014.

----------. *Saint Cyprian: Saint of Necromancers*. Hadean Press, 2011.

BREZSNY, Rob. *Pronoia is the Antidote for Paranoia: How the Whole World Is Conspiring to Shower You With Blessings*. North Atlantic Books, 2009.

COLEMAN, Martin. *Communing with the Spirits*. Xlibris, 2005.

E., Dr. *Working with Ancestors in Espiritismo*. Santeria Church of the Orishas. http://santeriachurch.org/working-with-ancestors-in-espiritismo, 2014.

EXCELSIOR, Kast et al. *Favourite Money Spells*. Pamphlet. Missionary Independent Spiritual Church, 2014.

HASKINS, Jim. *Voodoo and Hoodoo*. Scarborough House Publishers, 1978.

HURSTON, Zora Neale. *Mules and Men*. J. B. Lippincot, 1935; Harper Collins, 1990.

HYATT, Harry Middleton. *Hoodoo - Conjuration - Witchcraft - Rootwork*. [Five Vols.] Memoirs of the Alma Egan Hyatt Foundation, 1970-1978.

LAFOREST, Aura. *Hoodoo Spiritual Baths: Cleansing Conjure with Washes and Waters*. Lucky Mojo Curio Co., 2014.

MICHAELE, Miss and Professor Charles Porterfield. *Hoodoo Bible Magic: Sacred Secrets of Scriptural Sorcery*. Missionary Independent Spiritual Church, 2014.

MICKAHARIC, Draja. *Spiritual Cleansing: A Handbook of Psychic Protection*. Samuel Weiser, 1982.

MILLER, Jason. *Financial Sorcery: Magical Strategies to Create Real and Lasting Wealth*. New Page Books, 2012.

MILLETT, Deacon. *Hoodoo Honey and Sugar Spells: Sweet Love Magic in the Conjure Tradition*. Lucky Mojo Curio Co., 2013.

----------. *Hoodoo Return and Reconciliation Spells: True Love Magic in the Conjure Tradition*. Lucky Mojo Curio Co., 2015.

PUCKETT, Newbell Niles. *Folk Beliefs of the Southern Negro*. University of North Carolina Press, 1926.

REICHER, Sophie. *Spiritual Protection: A Safety Manual for Energy Workers, Healers, and Psychics*. New Page Books, 2010.

SELIG, Godfrey A. *Secrets of the Psalms*. Dorene, 1958.

SICKAFUS, James A. *Papa Jim Magical Herb Book*. Papa Jim II Inc., 1985.

SOMÉ, Malidoma Patrice. *The Healing Wisdom of Africa*. Tarcher / Putnam. 1999.

YOUNG, Jason R. *Rituals of Resistance: African Atlantic Religion in Kongo and the Lowcountry South in the Era of Slavery*. Louisiana State University Press, 2007.

YRONWODE, catherine. *The Art of Hoodoo Candle Magic in Rootwork, Conjure and Spiritual Church Services*. Missionary Independent Spiritual Church, 2013.

----------, et al. *The Black Folder: Personal Communications on the Mastery of Hoodoo*, Missionary Independent Spiritual Church, 2013.

----------. *Hoodoo Herb and Root Magic: A Materia Magica of African-American Conjure*. Lucky Mojo Curio Co., 2002.

----------. *Hoodoo Rootwork Correspondence Course: A One-Year Series of Weekly Lectures in African-American Conjure*. Lucky Mojo Curio Co., 2006.